DESTINY

DESTINY

HEZEKIAH WALKER

W

WHITAKER
HOUSE

DESTINY: DREAM IT, DECLARE IT, DO IT!

ISBN: 0-88368-874-3
Printed in the United States of America
© 2003 by Hezekiah Walker

Whitaker House
30 Hunt Valley Circle
New Kensington, PA 15068
www.whitakerhouse.com

Library of Congress Cataloging-in-Publication Data

Walker, Hezekiah.
  Destiny : dream it, declare it, do it! / Hezekiah Walker.
     p. cm.
  ISBN 0-88368-874-3 (trade paper : alk. paper)
  1. Self-realization—Religious aspects—Christianity. I. Title.
  BV4598.2 .W34 2003
  243—dc21
                                2002156462

2 3 4 5 6 7 8 9 10 11 12 13 14 / 12 11 10 09 08 07 06 05 04 03

Dedication

To the memory of my mother Gladys Walker, who is missed dearly. You are gone but never forgotten.

Also to the entire Walker family, especially my sister Viola.

And to my beautiful daughter KyAsia.

Acknowledgments

To my Lord and my God, thank You for giving me the grace to complete this book that I pray will touch thousands of lives.

To Bishop George Bloomer, thank you for the encouragement to write this book and for your always open door.

To my three best friends—Bishop Eric McDaniels, Pastor Mitchell Taylor, and Pastor Chad Hinson—I love you all!

To Bishop Kenneth Moales, Sr., thank you for your vision.

To Bishop Charles Mellette, Evangelist Carolyn Showell, Pastor Jackie McCullough, Evangelist Juanita Bynum, and Bishop George Seawright, thank you for your prayers and support.

To Charlie Ward and Allan Houston, thank you for all your encouragement.

To the Love Fellowship Tabernacle: The Kingdom Church family, I love you! Thank you for standing with me in the vision. This book is a part of you.

To all my fans, may this book excite you to move toward destiny!

To all my young people, both in New York and Pennsylvania, my love for you is beyond words.

Contents

Foreword

Foreword

The public housing projects in Brooklyn that Hezekiah Walker once called home are all too familiar to me. I lived not far from him in one of the other run-down city developments. His older brother was actually my downstairs neighbor. So, I know firsthand the kind of life that Hezekiah faced as a little boy growing up in that oppressive environment. It was the sort of existence that could suck the life right out of you if you didn't have something to live for. I saw so many people who walked around those projects in a sort of living death, with no hope for the future and no motivation to break free from the bondage the enemy had them in.

Hezekiah broke free in a big way because he had a dream in his heart. It was a dream to fulfill God's destiny for his life by becoming a minister to the masses. That dream, birthed in a little boy's believing heart, drove him to keep climbing toward his destiny, no matter how long the odds were. Hezekiah let his passion for singing carry him right out of the projects and into the national spotlight of gospel music. Along with the Love Fellowship Choir, Hezekiah has experienced the highest of highs in life on the musical stage. But that's not all.

Hezekiah's hunger for God pushed him to become a student of the Bible as he drew closer to the Lord each day. Now, he pastors a church that has congregations in two states with one more in the works in yet another state. It almost seems too good to be true for this man who was once just a poor boy living in the Brooklyn projects.

But true is exactly what it is. Hezekiah knows what he's talking about when he speaks of heartache, trials, pain from the past, betrayal, and paralyzing fear. He's been there, and, just like all of us, he still faces obstacles that the enemy wants to use to stop him from staying on his path to destiny.

But Hezekiah doesn't let the enemy stop him. And he doesn't want the enemy to stop you, either. That's the reason for this book you hold in your hands. Hezekiah has a message burning in his heart. It's a message of hope. It's a message of encouragement. It's a message that many people need to hear because they have been wondering for a long time what God is going to do with their lives.

Hezekiah is someone I have called a friend since our days as young teenagers in the projects. I know him well, and I know that the words he has to offer in this book are words that the church needs to hear today. Let Hezekiah point you to your destiny in the Lord. Along the way, remember that you are not reading the wisdom of a man who came down from some ivory tower to share his insights with humanity. You are learning from a man who has been through the fire and has come forth as gold! So, go with Hezekiah on a journey that

Destiny

will help you discover your destiny so that you can dream it, declare it, and do it!

Bishop George G. Bloomer
Senior Pastor, Bethel Family Worship Center
Durham, North Carolina

One

Purpose by Design

1
Purpose by Design

And we know that all things work together for good to them that love God, to them who are the called according to his purpose. For whom he did foreknow, he also did predestinate to be conformed to the image of his Son, that he might be the firstborn among many brethren. Moreover whom he did predestinate, them he also called: and whom he called, them he also justified: and whom he justified, them he also glorified.
—Romans 8:28–30

I t's a Saturday night in New York City, and I'm standing with the Love Fellowship Choir behind the center stage curtain at Radio City Music Hall, ready to cut yet another live album. I face the mammoth curtain on the dimly lit stage with my back to the choir, and I listen to the sounds coming from the six thousand fans who have come out tonight.

My heart begins to beat a little faster than normal as I hear the excitement of all the people in the audience.

They're ready to be a part of this historic night as we record the first live gospel album ever at Radio City Music Hall.

I close my eyes, breathe deeply, and try to take everything in. But it's all so overwhelming...

Actually doing a live recording on one of the greatest stages of all time...

Hearing the excitement of so many fans ready to cheer us on as soon as the curtain goes up...

Almost crying when I saw my name on the marquee outside as I arrived tonight...

Like I said: overwhelming!

I open my eyes, only to hear the buzz of the crowd cease. Seconds later, a pumped-up voice cuts sharply through the rising applause: "Live at Radio City Music Hall: Hezekiah Walker and the Love Fellowship Choir! Come on, give God praise!"

The curtain rises in front of me, and I am greeted by a raucous ovation that reverberates throughout the hall. The people are cheering and calling out my name as the band begins to play the intro to the song "We Made It." It's a tune that could be considered the theme song of every native New Yorker here tonight, being that it's been only five months since the 9/11 tragedy hit our city and nation.

I raise the microphone to my lips.

"Clap your hands, everybody! Come on!" I shout.

The crowd obliges and begins clapping to the rhythm of the music. I push them a little further.

"Y'all make some noise up in here. Come on!" I yell. "Let me hear you, New York! Come on!"

Loud cheers and shouts of joy follow, and I'm ready to sing. I jump right into the song, singing, "We made it, we survived." The choir comes in right after me, repeating the same lyrics until everyone in the audience joins in. As I let the words flow out of my spirit and into the microphone, I look out over the crowd. I think to myself, *The people are loving it!* At the height of the song, the entire crowd jumps into the rhythm of the hand-clapping, foot-stomping melody as we lift our voices together to let the enemy know that we made it. I know for sure that this is going to be an unforgettable night.

What a sight to see! The people are really into it. They're singing. They're dancing. They're clapping. The atmosphere is filled with the joy of the Lord.

The little boy inside me smiles and laughs with excitement. I can hear him in the back of my mind as I keep singing.

"Wow!" he says to me. *"I can't believe this! Look at all these people! Look at those bright lights! Listen to the crowd! The music sounds so wonderful, this almost seems like it's not real. It's like something right out of a dream!*

"You're really doing a live gospel recording here at Radio City Music Hall! Can you believe that you're making history tonight? Mmmm, gospel music has never been recorded here," the little boys says.

I want to let that little boy out of me so bad. I want to let him run around through the crowd and let him dance up and down the aisle singing as loud as he can, because that little boy in me is the same little boy who saw all this happening so long ago when things weren't so good.

Hello, Hardship

It was a quiet day, a lonely day, in Brooklyn's Fort Greene public housing project, one of the toughest, most drug-infested projects in the city at that time. I sat on the living room couch in our apartment, just a little eight-year-old boy who didn't know what the future held. Of course, things had gotten more confused just six months before my eighth birthday when my dad left. It was an eerie day that still haunted my mind as one of bittersweet relief. Sure, life hadn't been easy with my dad around, what with the tension between him and my mom, but when he was there, at least we were all together, dealing with life as it related to our family. My parents' relationship didn't exactly make for some story-book romance. It seemed as if their love had finally just fallen through the cracks, so my dad left.

Now, six months later, I sat on the couch depressed, fighting to answer the questions that raged in my mind. How were things going to be? Could my mom handle raising us children on her own? Could she be our protector in such a rough and tough environment?

As I stared out into the street through the living room window that day pondering these questions, I knew somehow that Mom could do it. I had seen her make sure we were fed and clothed. I had seen her cry at night, asking God to keep her children safe while she was out of the house. I knew she would come through for us, and I knew it was more than just providing for our physical needs.

When she wasn't working or out looking for work, my mom was doing all she could to instill in us her strong faith and trust in God. She read the Bible to us, and she stayed in constant prayer for all of us. There were the Saturdays when we had our own little church service for our family in the living room (naturally, I was the soloist). But more special to me were the times she would dig out a gospel album and play it for us. She would turn up the volume so loud that the music saturated our apartment, until the family who lived beneath us would start banging on their ceiling and my mom would finally have to turn it down. I'd watch as my mother at first sang along in tears of grief, but soon she would be swept away from the anger and injustice she felt into a place of love and peace and joy in the Holy Ghost.

> In God's presence, I knew I was safe and secure in His arms.

Then, the gospel singing bug would bite me, too, and I would be caught up in the music, in the words of Mahalia Jackson and Andrae Crouch and the Reverend James Cleveland and many others. I would find myself singing everywhere—in the bathroom, in the elevators, in the hallways. Eventually, everyone knew when I was coming because they could hear me singing a mile away. But I didn't care. Every time I sang gospel music, I had a peace about the future, and I knew I didn't have to think about anything because I was in God's care. In His presence, I knew I was safe and secure in His arms. Everything made sense in that perfect place.

Yet as I sat on our old couch, gazing out the window, I didn't feel like I was in any kind of perfect place in life. Why was my mom, a strong Christian, struggling to make ends meet for her family? She had taught my brother and sisters and me to believe that God would provide as long as we trusted Him, and we believed it. But if that were true, then why was life still so hard? Why did life seem so unfair? Why were other people who weren't Christians a lot better off than we were?

Not only that, but my father was still gone. I wished he were here now to help show me the way. I had so many questions: What does it mean to grow up and be a man? How do I become a man? Is a man supposed to get married, have kids, and be happy, or what? These questions flooded my mind and jabbed at my heart. Just like always, there was no one to answer my questions.

I continued to stare out through the window at a row of trees that blocked my view of the empty street. Suddenly, the trees were gone, and the street wasn't empty anymore. A vision danced in my mind's eye. The street was filled with blocks of people all listening to someone minister to them. I realized that the "someone" was me, even though I couldn't quite tell if I was singing or preaching. All those people were there to hear what God wanted me to tell them.

Then, as clear as a bell, came God's voice: "I'm going to make you great before men." I blinked, and the vision was gone. But I'd never forget those words. Rising from the couch that day, I knew that I had just seen who I could be, who God had called me to be. It was His plan, His blueprint for my life. Suddenly, my life started to make sense.

From Vision to Reality

Life may have started to make sense for me, but that didn't mean things were easier. I still had doubts and fears, I still didn't have my father around, and I still was just a poor little black boy from the Brooklyn projects. But I didn't let any of that stop my dream or the vision God had given me as a little boy. So, I started singing. And, of course, I sang gospel music.

Along the way, there were people who told me that I should forget my dream, that it couldn't be done, that I was going to be stuck in the projects and live out the same hopeless cycle of life that they were living—born into poverty, raised in poverty, eventually becoming an adult who fell into the evils of life such as drugs or violence and then lived in even more poverty. But it didn't matter what people said to me because, even when I had my doubts and fears, I kept pushing toward the vision God had given me. I knew that whether it was singing or preaching or both, it was my destiny.

"Let the enemy try to stop God's plan for my life," I said.

After all, the devil had tried before.

Oh, yes. The enemy was there when I was born three months premature and given no hope of survival. The enemy watched as I lay there in the hospital for nearly a year, a fragile little baby boy who was the weakest of the weak. But my mom wouldn't stop believing, and God sent her a reassuring word. A group of her friends from church prophesied that I would be anointed of God to be used in the latter days. Mom believed the prophecy, and she cried out in prayer for God to raise me up from my sickbed. The enemy's attempt to stop my destiny failed as I came home from the hospital and grew into a healthy little boy.

The enemy was there that haunting day when my father left us. He watched as I sat in silent shock, not knowing whether I should be happy or sad that my father was gone. The enemy plagued my mind with fears and doubts about the future. And what a bleak future it was, according to the enemy! But God had destined me to sing to the masses, and the enemy's attempt to stop my destiny failed as I began to sing along with my mother's gospel music and lift myself above the hurt and pain and into God's perfect presence.

The enemy was there that day I sat on the couch, thinking about this fear and that fear. He made sure I doubted the kind of life I could have and the kind of man I could become. But God had destined me to rise up into true manhood and discover my destiny. The enemy's attempt to block my destiny that day failed as I received God's vision for my future and accepted His call for my life.

I kept following that call, too, as I began to sing with the Love Fellowship Choir and we recorded our first album. Then came a second and a third album and many more. We traveled all over the nation and across the globe, as well. And then we started a church in Brooklyn. We began the Love Fellowship Tabernacle with eight members, and we have seen it grow and move from one building to another to accommodate all the new people who come through its doors to hear the Gospel. Then we started another church in Pennsylvania, and the same explosion in attendance that we saw in New York happened in the new church, too. Now, another church in Newark, New Jersey, is on the way.

I'm preaching every chance I get, but I've never quit singing with the Love Fellowship Choir. Everywhere I go to sing and preach, I can't escape the vision the Lord gave me when I was just eight years old. But now, I can look back and see how God brought me from destiny to fulfillment. I can see that God's plan was there all the times when I struggled and scrapped and scraped my way through life. There have been many valleys in my life, but there have been so many wonderful mountaintops, as well. Along the way, I wanted to throw in the towel more than once, but the vision kept me going. I had my destiny in my sight, and I didn't give up.

The rewards have been more than just singing and preaching to the masses. I have seen countless lives touched by the power of God. I have been blessed by the friends and family who have stood with me through it all, and I know that they were there as part of God's plan for my life.

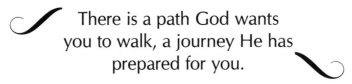

There is a path God wants you to walk, a journey He has prepared for you.

My life is so much more than just some rags-to-riches story that sounds too good to be true. I understand that God has given me a destiny to fulfill. When I'm on the stage singing or preaching, it feels exactly right. I have such a peaceful feeling knowing that this is what God has called me to do—that I was created to minister to the masses and help bring them into God's presence. I have a sense of destiny, and I know that He planned for me to walk this path even before I was born.

I want you to know that He has designed a destiny for your life, as well. There is a path He wants you to walk, a journey He has prepared for you. I've seen Him work in my life to keep me on the destined path He chose for me. And what God has done in my life, He wants to do in yours, too!

Destiny Is Calling—Will You Answer?

I don't know who you are. I don't know where you came from. I don't know what fears you have about life or about your future. But I do know that God cares about you and that He has a plan, a blueprint, for your life, even though it may not take you in the same direction or along the same path as mine. Romans 8:28–30 says that God foreknew us, meaning He already knew all about us even before we were born. It also says that, as believers, He predestinated us to be like His Son and that He called us. That means He has a plan for our lives as we walk in our faith and become more like Jesus Christ. Perhaps the greatest thing to draw from these verses is the meaning of the Greek word that is translated *"predestinate"* (v. 29). In the original language, this word means "to be decided upon beforehand." Did you catch that? It means that God decided each of our callings—our paths in life—before we even came out of the womb!

It doesn't matter what you do for a living, either, because when you are doing what you are called to do, the anointing will break forth from you as the Holy Spirit sees fit. Whether you are a gospel singer or a teacher or a truck driver or a homemaker, if the anointing is there and you are abiding in it, you can do as much as anyone else in the body of Christ.

In England many years ago, Smith Wigglesworth followed his anointing, and he had a ministry so powerful that God used him to raise twenty or so people from the dead. Wigglesworth, by the way, was a plumber.

Destiny

See, it doesn't matter who you are or what you do. We can't sit back and judge that one person's destiny is great or small. Every person's destiny is great in the eyes of the Lord because God has a purpose for everyone.

Remember that. God has a plan for your life, and that plan cannot be stopped as long as you rest in the anointing. The call God has placed upon your life is real, and He wants to see you walk the path He has laid out for you. Knowing what this divine destiny is will make all the difference in your life.

When you realize that God foreknew and predestinated you (Rom. 8:29), then you can understand that He has a plan for your life. When you understand that, you can't help but have a deep peace within, knowing that God has called you to walk in His anointing toward your individual destiny and achieve all that He has planned for you. You can know without a shadow of a doubt that you have purpose in life. Purpose, in turn, becomes your driving force as you move toward your divine destiny.

However, if you think the enemy will sit idly by and watch you fulfill your destiny, you're dead wrong. Satan will come at you with everything he has: fears, doubts, hatred, jealousy, heartache, regrets, pain from the past, people who betray you, and so much more. It's up to you to stand strong and battle the enemy at every turn on your destined path. It's up to you to completely surrender to God and wait patiently for Him as He continues to shape and mold you with every trial and tribulation you go through. It's up to you to keep your eyes on His plan for your life and to keep an eternal perspective about what goes on around you, knowing that your final glorious destiny awaits you in heaven. Remember, no obstacle can stop you from reaching your destiny here on earth if you persevere to live out your call from God—even obstacles that seem to lead you away from the path that the Lord has placed you on. (See Romans 8:28.) God planned the way He is taking us, and after you have been tried in the fires of suffering and trials, you shall come forth as pure gold (Job 23:10).

Riding the Rough Road of Life

Scripture gives us a good lesson about the path of destiny in the book of Genesis. Joseph, Jacob's son, was the next-to-youngest in a family of twelve boys. He probably realized early on that he was going to have it pretty rough, since he was one of the runts of the bunch. It didn't help, either, that he was Jacob's favorite son. The special coat that Jacob gave to him did little to endear him to his brothers, who just found one more reason to hate him.

Things certainly didn't get any easier when Joseph began to understand that God had a purpose and plan for his life. One night, he had a dream. He knew the dream was from God, for in the dream, he came to understand that he would someday rise above all his brothers and that they would bow before him.

Joseph didn't help his cause when he told all his brothers about the dream. Their hatred for him grew even more. The next morning, Joseph went ahead and told them about another dream he had. In this one, not only his brothers bowed before him, but also his mother and father. Guess what? Dad was sitting there listening to Joseph's story this time, and he wasn't exactly thrilled with his favorite son, either. Still, even though

Joseph's brothers despised him all the more, his father took note of what his son said about his future.

One day, Joseph's father sent him to check on his brothers, who were working in the fields. Joseph went to find his brothers, not knowing that the enemy had laid a trap for him in an attempt to stop him from fulfilling God's plan for his life. The story probably played out like this: As Joseph came over a ridge, his brothers spotted him.

"Here comes that arrogant little dreamer," they muttered, playing right into the hands of the enemy.

Finally, Joseph reached his brothers and greeted them. At that moment, his life took a change for the worse. He was snatched up, stripped of his special coat, and thrown into a pit. All the while, his brothers breathed out murderous threats. Joseph stayed at the bottom of the pit while his brothers sat eating supper and figuring out how they should murder him. When a group of traders rode by, one of the brothers convinced the rest to sell Joseph into slavery rather than kill him. Soon, Jacob's favorite son was on his way to Egypt as the property of a band of nomads. Meanwhile, Jacob was being shown his beloved son's special coat, which Joseph's brothers had torn apart and dipped in goat's blood to make their father believe that Joseph had been mangled by a wild animal. Jacob practically had a heart attack when he saw the coat and imagined the horrible death Joseph supposedly endured. And off Jacob went in his grief.

In Egypt, Joseph was sold into slavery as a servant of Potiphar, one of the nation's officials. Still, Joseph wouldn't let his faith in God die, and God watched over him and granted him favor in Potiphar's eyes. Soon,

Potiphar entrusted Joseph with the care of his whole household, and the Lord blessed the Egyptian and all his affairs because of Joseph.

The enemy, though, had other plans for Joseph, plans to derail him from his destiny.

Potiphar's wife found Joseph to be an attractive young man, and she attempted to seduce him time and again. Joseph refused her every time, choosing to stay on the righteous path God had placed him on. One fateful day, though, after resisting another of her seductions, Joseph fled from Potiphar's house. Soon, he was dragged back and accused of trying to have his way with Potiphar's wife. Guess who made the accusation? The master's wife, an unwitting pawn in the hands of the enemy!

Potiphar came home and was told the story of the "evil" Joseph had committed. His blood boiled as the tale was told, and he had Joseph cast into prison. Once again, Joseph's life seemed to have taken a turn for the worse. How could God possibly work all this out toward accomplishing Joseph's destiny?

In spite of the raw deal he was given, Joseph held on to his faith in God. After a short while, God again granted him favor, this time in the eyes of the jailer, who allowed Joseph to run the prison for him.

Later on, two prisoners were jailed for crimes against Pharaoh, the king of Egypt. Each of the prisoners then had a dream he couldn't understand, and God granted Joseph the ability to interpret the dreams for them. Eventually, one prisoner was executed, but the other was restored to his previous position, just as Joseph had told them would happen based on their dreams. Not wanting to miss a chance at freedom, Joseph told the

Destiny

freed prisoner to put in a good word for him when he returned to Pharaoh.

The prisoner didn't.

Two years passed. Joseph persisted in his faith in God even though he was still a prisoner in a foreign land. Finally, the freed prisoner remembered Joseph after hearing that the king had dreamed a dream that no one could interpret. Joseph was quickly hauled out of jail and cleaned up on orders from Pharaoh. He was placed before the Egyptian king, the most powerful mortal in the known world, and told to interpret his dream for him.

Joseph listened as Pharaoh recounted his dream. Then he explained to the great king that a severe famine loomed for the nation and that Egypt needed to take action immediately to save itself during the lean years to come. Pharaoh, amazed at the young Hebrew's wisdom and keen insight, appointed Joseph as his second-in-command, lord of the land of Egypt and master of all except Pharaoh. He was also given charge of insuring that Egypt would not starve during the coming time of famine, and that is exactly what Joseph did, using the wisdom that God gave him.

Soon, the famine came, just as Joseph had said it would. However, Egypt was prepared—so prepared that people started coming from neighboring lands to buy food. Joseph sat and watched as band after band of foreigners came to buy from him. One day, his gaze rested on a group of men whom he instantly recognized, even after all those years. His brothers had come to Egypt to buy food, and here they were bowing down to him, in fulfillment of his dreams! Joseph hid his identity from them in order to test them and see if they had changed.

When they showed that they had, Joseph revealed himself to them and forgave them, bringing about reconciliation. Then Joseph summed up his destined journey from slave to lord in one incredible statement: *"You meant evil against me; but God meant it for good"* (Gen. 50:20 NKJV).

A Lesson to Learn

Another rags-to-riches story that's almost unbelievable, right? Not at all, because Joseph understood that he had a divine destiny, so he persevered through the toughest of times.

Let's think about Joseph. Here we have a boy who knew from an early age a little about the plan God had for his life. He may have been too quick to tell people about it when perhaps he should have kept it as something special between God and himself. This little mistake seemed to allow the enemy to get a shot at him and knock him off his destined path. Satan might have succeeded, too, but Joseph never wavered in his faith in God. Satan kept throwing obstacles in Joseph's path of destiny, but Joseph just kept plowing ahead, knowing that God's plan would come to pass if he stayed the course.

Joseph almost could have thanked the enemy for the obstacles, for little did the devil know that he was merely helping Joseph reach his destined place, the place he had seen in his dreams as a boy. Hindsight, of course, would prove to be 20/20 when Joseph looked back on his life and he could say, "Oh yeah, I see how God used that trial and that pain to get me to where I am today!" Don't think, though, that the obstacles he faced weren't real. If Joseph had chosen to turn from

God at any point, he would have found himself in a place of confusion, pain, and regret. Instead, he chose the path of destiny and lived to see all that God had planned for him.

We can do no less! If we are unsure of what God's plans for our lives are, we need to seek His face and find out the destinies He is calling us to. If we already have even an inkling of our divine destinies, then we must go for them with all our strength, for they are attainable, despite what the enemy will try to do to get us offtrack. Obviously, there are things we can learn from God's Word and from the lives of those who have gone before us that can help us on our destined journeys. I have written this book so that, together, we can find out how best to walk on the paths that lead us to our divine destinies.

> If we are unsure of what God's plans are, we need to seek His face.

Our journey in this book will reveal many of the pitfalls we will inevitably face as we seek to achieve our destinies in Christ. We'll also examine the way change affects our lives and how it is painful yet so necessary in our growth as Christian men and women.

We'll learn that the past is the past, but that this is one area the devil will use to try to get our focus off our destinies. The future, of course, plays a very important part in our destiny, and when we have a grasp of it, we can better handle the past and live in the present. We will find out that faith dictates what we will do about our futures and how willing we are to seize the moment day by day.

We will also explore how the things that attract us in life are not always the best things for us, and how, even when we fall prey to one of these "fatal attractions," we can still learn from it and use it on our way to our destinies.

Another critical area we will look into together is that of the people who surround us. Often, the very people whom we trust implicitly are the ones who turn around and betray us, not knowing that they are tools in the hands of the enemy as he unceasingly tries to hinder our journeys toward destiny. On the other hand, we will see that there are friends and members of our families who will be giant boosts to our confidence and who will be faithful supporters throughout our walk with God. They will lift us up through each step of our calling, and they will not be jealous of our achievements.

Another vital area that we will explore is that of fear. Fear is such a powerful weapon in the enemy's hand. We must learn to combat it if we are to seize our destiny. In addition, we must be careful with all our feelings because they can dominate our lives and detour us from our destinies. When we are skillful in dealing with our feelings, they can be of great benefit to us and help us stay strong when our destinies seem hopelessly out of reach. Conversely, when we let our feelings get the best of us, especially those negative feelings such as worry and doubt, then the enemy will gain a foothold in our lives and begin to maneuver us away from God's plans.

Finally, we will find out just what it takes to achieve success in life. Even more than that, though, we will learn to seize the opportunity when success is within reach and discover how to maintain success as we come to understand how it fits in with God's master blueprint for our lives.

By looking at Scripture and experiences from my own life and from the lives of others, we will together come to see that all of us do indeed have a purpose in life, a divine destiny that we can move toward if we keep the faith. This knowledge can enable us to move out of the so-called safe harbors of life and set sail with the determination that nothing is going to stand in the way of our achieving our destinies on this earth!

Remember, it's your destiny. Dream it, declare it, and then do it!

Two

Discovering Destiny

2
Discovering Destiny

But He knows the way that I take.
—Job 23:10 (NKJV)

H ave you ever heard people talk about having a "burning bush experience"? Most of us know the story behind the expression. It's from the life of Moses.

Moses, who had fled from Egypt years before, was tending his father-in-law's sheep in the desert one day when something caught his eye. A bush in the distance was on fire. Moses stared at it, waiting for it to burn up, but it never did. Finally, Moses decided to walk over and see why the fire wasn't consuming this bush. As he approached the bush, a voice called to him from out of the middle of the fire. It was God, telling Moses to go back to Egypt and free his people from the bonds of their slavery. After struggling against the command of God, Moses finally went and did what God told him to do, fulfilling the destiny that the Lord had for his life. (See Exodus 3:1–4:20.)

My point in telling this story is that Moses had a clear calling from God. Even though he struggled with God's divine plan for his life, he knew he had to obey the voice of God. He was much like Joseph, whom we talked about in the last chapter. Joseph knew God's destiny for his life after the Lord gave him two dreams that pointed him to his destiny. In my own life, the vision I had when I was eight years old did the same thing for me. It pointed me to what I knew to be my divine destiny.

No doubt, some of you have had a similar experience. You've had a dream or a vision or some other sort of "burning bush experience" that has helped direct you to God's calling for your life. But I also know that others of you are thinking, "That's nice that all these people get a clear sign from God about what they're supposed to be doing in life. But what about me? God hasn't given me a vision, and I haven't seen any burning bushes!"

Don't panic! Just because you don't feel that God has revealed His destiny for your life doesn't mean you don't have one. In this chapter, we're going to look at how you can discover the destiny that God has for your life. Even if you already have a clear sense of your destiny, this look at the keys to unlocking your destiny in God can help reconfirm the call God has placed on your life.

Tune In to Your Talents

While there are several keys that can help you discover your divine destiny, three major ones can help the most in your search for purpose in life. The first of these is the combination of skills and abilities God has given to you. All of us have something we're good at, no matter what it might be. Maybe you're good with children. Maybe you're good at speaking in front of people. Perhaps you're good with your hands and can craft things that few people can. Or maybe you can whip through mathematical problems with ease. The list could go on and on. The point is that every single one of us has something that we are good at, something that takes skills and abilities that we obviously possess.

I believe that the talents we have in life are gifts from God. Not only that, but I also know that many times these talents end up being what God uses in His destiny for our lives. Consider the example of Daniel in the Old Testament. Daniel had lived in Judah when he was a young man, perhaps a teen, during the time the kingdom of Babylon invaded the Hebrew land and conquered it. In those days, it was customary for conquering nations to search through the captives of the defeated land looking for anyone who showed unusual wisdom and ability. You guessed it: Daniel was the man. The Bible refers to Daniel as a man who was *"gifted in all wisdom, possessing knowledge and quick to understand"* (Dan. 1:4 NKJV). Because of the abilities that God had blessed Daniel with, the Babylonians chose him to be among those who would serve the king himself in the palace.

Even though he was a royal official in Nebuchadnezzar's court, Daniel continued to serve God and to take a stand against the idolatry that was going on all around him. On several occasions, Daniel faced persecution because he followed God and surrendered himself to God's plan for his life. In each case, God came through and delivered Daniel. But more than that, God used Daniel's witness to glorify Himself among the false gods of the heathen kings and to turn the hearts of these kings away from their idolatrous beliefs.

In addition, because of Daniel's great knowledge, he was able to help when it came to giving the kings information that no one else could. So, he was often a fixture in the palaces, and his witness, more than likely, was something that no one could help but notice. Daniel also had a prophetic gift; he foretold events that would not take place for many years. Looking back, we can verify that Daniel was right on the money in all he predicted.

I doubt that Daniel knew as a little boy that he would someday be a witness for God in the palace of heathen kings or that he would command so much respect from those same kings. The point is that Daniel used the abilities God had given him, and he stayed faithful to the Lord. In this way, Daniel saw God's destiny for his life unfold before his eyes.

And what about Joshua? Here was a Hebrew who was freed with the rest of the Israelites when Moses delivered them from enslavement to the Egyptians. Somewhere along the line, Joshua was picked by Moses to lead a group of soldiers and to fight against one of the enemies of Israel. He helped lead the Israelites to victory that day. (See Exodus 17:8–16.) Joshua is later listed as Moses' assistant, one of his *"choice men"* (Num. 11:28 NKJV). Joshua was also chosen as the representative of his tribe to go to the Promised Land when Moses sent spies there to search out the territory. (See Numbers 13–14.)

It seems to me that, at some point in Joshua's life, he was noticed by those above him as having the ability to lead. Obviously, Moses noticed this quality and made sure that Joshua was in a position where he could best use his skills and talents. It's also clear that Joshua stayed strong in his commitment to the Lord, as only he and Caleb trusted God enough to want to go right into the Promised Land and conquer it in the name of the Lord. (See Numbers 14:6–9.) It was this commitment to the Lord that brought Joshua into the divine destiny for his life.

When it was time for Moses to appoint a successor to lead the Israelites, God told him Joshua would lead the nation into the Promised Land (Deut. 1:38). You may know the rest of the story. Joshua took command of the Israelites, and God brought him victory after victory in the Promised Land so that the Israelites finally had their own nation, just as God had promised Abraham long ago.

> We can discover the divine design for our lives by looking at the gifts God has given us.

Again, it is apparent that Joshua had certain abilities that carried him toward his destiny in God. The same could be said of David, who was a shepherd as a boy, someone who understood directing and moving a flock and also what it took to protect sheep from enemies. God called this young shepherd boy to be the king of Israel, a shepherd of the Hebrew people and a warrior who fought against the enemies of God.

Now, I don't know what you are good at, or what skills and abilities you have. But I do know that if you're not really sure about where you fit into the kingdom of God and what the Lord's plan for your life is, then you can look to your talents as something that may point you to God's plan for your life. I'm not saying that, just because you're good at something, God has to use it as the main focus of your destiny. But I am saying that we can often discover the divine design for our lives by looking at the gifts God has given us. In any case, even if we do begin to see where God is calling us, it is still up to us to seize our destinies by faith and by surrendering our lives to Him. So, if you feel lost when it comes to your calling, be faithful where God has placed you, and use the skills He has given you to glorify Him in all you do. He will, in turn, be faithful to show you the plan for your life in His perfect time.

Passion with a Purpose

Another area that can help point us to our divine destiny is the things we are passionate about in life. Now, this is a little different from your talents and abilities. You can have a talent for something but not be passionate about it. Passions in life can be just strong desires we have to do or accomplish something, with no ties at all to our talents. Many times, passions end up working hand in hand with talents, but passions by themselves can also lead us to our destiny.

Think about it in this way. A little girl may love watching her mother bake. Eventually, this girl may become passionate about the idea of being a great chef someday. She just loves the idea of being in the kitchen, with the aroma of good food in the air. Now, at this point, she may not have any ability to bake or cook at all. But if she does the work and follows her passion, the skill will come. She may also come to find that such a passion carried her right into God's plan for her life.

As Christians, we often have passions that have nothing to do with our abilities. We may be passionate about seeing people won to the Lord, even though we don't really like talking to people. We may be passionate about helping kids succeed in school, even though we've never taught before. As with skills and abilities, the list of passions could go on and on. The point is that our strong desires in life can often propel us into what God has called us to do.

I think of when I was a little boy who loved listening to gospel music. I would get so excited about the music that I knew it was something I wanted to be involved with someday. But I hadn't sung yet, and I didn't even know if I was good at it. Singing was just a passion that burned in my heart. God took that passion and turned it into a desire to learn to sing. Eventually, I acquired the skills and abilities I needed to live out my destiny in Him.

Moses had a similar experience. As we saw earlier, he received a clear picture of his destiny when God spoke to him from the burning bush. Years earlier, though, it was Moses' passion for his Hebrew brothers and sisters that got him in trouble with Pharaoh. As Pharaoh's adopted son, Moses had it good in life. He knew he was a Hebrew, but he lived a life of royalty while the rest of the Israelites slaved away for the Egyptians. Finally, though, Moses' zeal for his people got the better of him. One day, he went out to see the children of Israel toiling in the sun, and he watched as they performed their backbreaking work. Then, he saw an Egyptian beating a Hebrew, and he couldn't stand to sit by and watch. He ran over and struck the Egyptian, killing him on the spot. Pharaoh eventually found out and wanted Moses dead. It was then that Moses fled into the desert and lived as a shepherd. (See Exodus 2:11–22.)

Moses had a passion to see his brothers and sisters freed from their oppression. The only problem was that he took matters into his own hands and let his zeal rule his life when he killed the Egyptian. But years later, when Moses stood in front of the burning bush, God turned that passion into Moses' destiny. A short time later, Moses returned to Egypt, and he eventually saw God deliver the Israelites from the Egyptians. Moses, by his own admission, may not have been the most skilled speaker or leader of people. Yet God gave Moses the tools he needed when it came to using his zeal to accomplish his destiny.

The apostle Paul also found himself living out his divine destiny after God turned his passion into a plan for his life. Paul, then called Saul, was zealous in his desire to learn God's law (Acts 22:3). So strong was his passion to follow God's rules and regulations that he persecuted and killed followers of Jesus because he felt it necessary to stamp out such "heretics" (Acts 9:1–2; 22:4). Then, one day, God got hold of Paul and showed him the light (Acts 9:3–19).

Paul immediately turned his zeal for the law into a weapon of evangelism. He passionately preached Christ to other Jews, reasoning with them from the Old Testament and showing them how Christ was indeed the Messiah (verses 20–22). Then, God turned Paul to the Gentiles and used his passion for preaching to bring the message of the Gospel to those who had never heard it. (See Acts 26:16–20.)

It may be the same with you. Maybe there's something in life that you love with a passion that can't be stopped. Maybe it's something you even think is small and trivial, something like writing poetry or gardening or playing baseball. And maybe it's not something you're really good at—yet. God can take that passion and use it to achieve His divine destiny for your life. He'll give you the tools you need to see the thing accomplished. You just need to be sensitive to His leading and recognize that the passion you have could in fact be what God has planned as your destiny. At that point, you need to go after it and get it!

Dreams Do Matter

Did you ever daydream when you were a kid? You'd be sitting in class, maybe, and thinking, "Boy, I'd really like to be a doctor someday!" or "I'd like to be an astronaut!" You get the idea. I'm sure we all have done this at some point in our lives. Most of the time, though, we dismiss such seemingly fantastic thoughts and go on our way. I want to tell you that dreams like those do matter because they may very well be the destiny God has planned for your life.

Dreams can be birthed out of many things. They may come from our being really good at something, as we discussed earlier. Or, as we also talked about, they may come from a passion in life that we have. They may come from our watching a television show and seeing something that we'd really like to be. It doesn't matter where the dreams come from. What does matter is that dreams are important.

I think again of when I wanted to be a singer. Oh, I had a vision about it already. However, the passion for singing helped me to have a dream about singing. And after I had the dream, I went after it. There were people around me who said I would never make it. They said I would never get out of the projects. They said it was impossible to do what I wanted to do with my life. It didn't matter to me what they said. I knew I had a dream, and I wanted to make it a reality. Fortunately, I had the support of my mom. She helped nurture my dream and make it a reality. Sadly, many people don't have parents like that.

Too often, little Timmy or Mary comes running home from school and shouting, "Hey, Mom! Hey, Dad! You know what I want to be when I grow up?" And when the parents hear that their little one wants to be a brain surgeon or a firefighter or Miss America, they say, "That's nice! Now, go out and play." What a tragedy!

It doesn't matter where dreams
come from—dreams are important.

Please understand that these dreams are real in the child's mind. Instead of dismissing such dreams as wild ideas, we should encourage children, and even adults, to go after their dreams. Those dreams may change fifty times in a month, especially in the case of children. But it doesn't matter. If we are supportive of such dreamers, we show them that their desires in life are important and that they are worth going after. Not only that, but the dreams may very well be their divine destinies.

Consider Joseph's experience again. He had a couple of dreams, not the kind of dreams we have, necessarily, but dreams that pointed to his divine destiny. His brothers and even his father laughed at him, yet it turned out that the dreams were indeed from God. Who is to say that a child's, or even an adult's, musings can't be a message from God concerning the destiny of that person? Now, I'm not saying that this is always the case. However, I am saying that we shouldn't just discard our dreams, or anyone else's, as though they were some silly thing that doesn't deserve a second look. Sometimes, they may very well turn out to be just whimsical fantasies that didn't really have any root. But, many times, these dreams can in fact become our destinies. That's why we need to stay in prayer about God's will for our lives. If our dreams are truly something that will become our destinies, then God will give us direction regarding them and will lead us down the right path.

Destiny for the Day

"That's all well and good, but I'm still not any closer to knowing what my destiny is!" you say. Well, don't get discouraged. You have a destiny that God wants you to fulfill whether you know what it is or not. If you really don't know what God is calling you to do, then I have one word of advice for you that actually is good for everyone to hear: Fulfill your destiny for the day. Whether you know what your destiny for tomorrow is or not, walk in God's will for your life today.

If we have peace about where we are in life, even if we don't know our destinies, we can rest in the fact that God will bring to pass what He promised, namely, ordering our steps in His perfect plan. (See Romans 4:20–21.) In other words, He will lead us down the right road even when we do not know where the road goes. This takes a commitment to God because, if we know we are in His will for the day, then we are moving toward our destinies, no matter what. It's not as if we have to have our destinies written out on a plaque to remind us where we're going. We know that our ultimate destiny is to be in heaven with God. Our journeys on the earth may be such that God asks us to live out each day in His plan for that particular day. So, don't be frustrated if you don't know where your journey is taking you. God will see to it that you fulfill your destiny; and if you continue to surrender to Him daily, He will begin to reveal His plan for your life little by little. Again, be faithful where you are right now, and God will bless you for it.

Also, don't get frustrated if you felt you were heading down destiny's path and then, all of a sudden, the thing you were doing fell apart. The devil will try to get us off our paths of destiny by attracting us to other things that we shouldn't go after. That's something we'll look at in a later chapter. However, what I'm talking about here is when you have a peace about what you are doing, and then it collapses in front of you, and you conclude that you must have missed God's call for your life. Not necessarily!

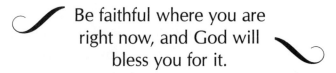

Be faithful where you are right now, and God will bless you for it.

Many times, God will show you a little bit of your destiny and then wait to reveal more of it to you until after you have faithfully stepped out in faith based on the knowledge you already have. Think about this example: A young man enters college with the goal of becoming a doctor. He feels very strongly that God has called him to be a physician who will research cures for cancer. After one year in school, though, he finds himself hating all the tedious lab work that is required. He wonders if he really ever heard from God. Realizing that he has to switch his field of study, he thinks about what he would like to do. He remembers how good it felt in his introductory English class to hear the teacher say that he showed promise as a newswriter. He imagines all the positive things he could do as a newswriter and decides to study journalism.

After graduation, the man goes on to become a successful reporter whose articles have an enormous impact on the community he lives in. He looks back and remembers the teacher who inspired him to write. More important, he remembers that, if he hadn't started off in premed, he never would have had the biology professor who highly recommended his enrolling in the English class taught by the teacher who started his dream of writing.

This man had been on God's path all along, even though it certainly didn't feel like it when he first recognized he wasn't meant to be a doctor. God may take us through steps to our destiny that do not make any sense to us. The key is to be faithful where he has called us, each and every day. If we are doing everything we can to grow as Christians and to become closer to God, He will see to it that His plans are being accomplished in us. In this way, we can know that we are on the path to God's destiny for our lives.

Set Your Compass

Whether we know our destinies or not, there is one thing we all must do to stay in God's will for our lives. That is to please Him every day. We need to stay connected to Him so that we can grow spiritually and then be used by Him wherever He places us at any given moment.

When people are out in the woods or mountains on an outdoor adventure, if they are smart, they know that they always need to keep a compass with them in case they get lost. If they have that compass, they can reorient themselves and find the way to their destination.

We need to keep our "compasses" pointed toward God by remembering Him every day and meditating on His promises to watch over us. He has a plan for our lives. Only by drawing as close to Him as we can will we be able to see, day by day, the unfolding of those plans.

Three

The Pain of Change

3
The Pain of Change

Why is my pain perpetual?
—Jeremiah 15:18

I remember a few years ago when a brother in our ministry started dating a young lady who attended our church. They were a pair to see. Everyone, including myself, thought they were the perfect match. They just fit together so well that it seemed clear to me and everyone around them that they were destined to be together. They dated for two years, but with no sign of an engagement on the horizon. Finally, I approached the young man and asked him about his relationship with the young lady. I told him that everyone was expecting him to make an announcement about their engagement. "She's waiting, I'm waiting, everyone is waiting to hear it!" I said. "Why don't you marry her?"

He explained that in the natural, she was all he could hope for. She was attractive, she was intelligent, she had finished college, and she had a good job. The problem, he said, was that during the two years they had dated, he had been watching her spiritual development. He shared how he was disappointed to see that this young lady was not maturing in her walk with Christ. So, even though they appeared to be the perfect couple and even though in church she appeared to be a strong Christian, he just knew they were not compatible spiritually.

He told me how he was struggling to end their relationship. He knew she wasn't meant to be a part of God's plan for his life, but, at the same time, he genuinely loved her and wanted her in his life. Finally, after much prayer, he did what he knew he had to do to stay in God's will. He ended the relationship.

This change brought him great pain. He was heartbroken and felt the bitter sting of severing a relationship with someone he truly wanted in his life. But that wasn't the only pain he felt. The young lady's family turned on him and accused him of stringing her along and using her. Members of the congregation also criticized him, saying that he was doing the wrong thing and that he and the girl were meant to be together.

The young man felt the pain, and I'm sure it must have cut him deeply. But I saw him continue to seek God's will for his life and to rest in the fact that he had done the right thing by letting the girl go. It wasn't long before the young man met another young lady in the church. This girl, in the natural, didn't appear at all to be someone who would be compatible with him, and people told him so. Again, a change in his life brought him pain. But, as before, he sought what God wanted for him, and he came to the determination that the girl he was now dating was the one for him. People told him she wasn't the right one, but he didn't listen, despite their painful words.

The man married the young lady, and I can tell you that he has grown spiritually by leaps and bounds since she entered his life. He is now a minister in our church, and I can see that his wife is a spiritual rock in his life, a vital support for him. She is someone he never would have shared his life with if he had let the pain others inflicted on him influence his decision to end his relationship with the other young lady. That young lady, by the way, has backslidden and grown weak in her faith.

The young man decided to follow God's plan for his life despite what others said and expected of him. When it was time to make a change, even though it was a very painful one, he did it, knowing that he was honoring God with that decision. And he is better off today for it because not only does he have a wife who is a perfect spiritual match for him, but he is also a more mature Christian and still on the path of destiny that God placed him on.

Change will come to all of us. Sometimes, we will be directly responsible for the change, while other times, things will change around us no matter what we do or don't do. Throughout our lives, we will face change in three major areas: in ourselves, in the people surrounding us, and in our situations in life. More than likely, each change will bring us some level of pain. Remember, though, that experiencing any level of pain can't compare with persevering through the suffering and rising to another level in Christ. With that in mind, let's take a look at the area of change in which we may very well experience the most pain: ourselves.

Take a Look in the Mirror

I heard the tale of a man from long ago who developed a daily ritual from which we can learn a valuable lesson. This man would rise early each morning, eat breakfast, and then dress in a finely tailored suit. Before stepping out the door, he would always stop in front of a full-length mirror—the only mirror in his house—and check his appearance. Each day, he would gaze at himself in the mirror and smile, thinking, "That's what's up!" (as the young people would say). Time went by, and because he knew he was the model of perfect appearance, he decided to take down the mirror and replace it with a large portrait of himself.

From then on, the man stopped in front of the portrait before he left for work. He'd smile and whisper, "The picture of perfection, eh?" Day after day, he did this, and all day long, he thought he looked like the man in the portrait. Then, one day, the man put on his shirt and noticed it didn't fit quite as nicely as it once had. The same went for his trousers. The man figured that he simply needed some newer clothing and went straight to his tailor. The tailor sized him up and told him his measurements. The man's jaw dropped. "Impossible!" he cried. "Where is a mirror?" The tailor pointed to one on the far wall of his shop.

The man walked quickly over to the mirror and looked at himself in the glass. He shook his head. "There's something wrong with your mirror!" he shouted at the tailor. "I don't look anything like myself in it. I just looked at my portrait this morning, and I looked the same as I always have!"

Change Your Ways

This story may seem silly to many of us. It does seem ridiculous for a man to measure himself by what he once was without allowing for the possibility of change.

The only problem is, we do the same thing all the time. I'm not necessarily talking about the way we view ourselves physically. I'm talking about the way we think, the way we handle ourselves emotionally, and the level of spirituality we maintain in our lives. Often, we become so set in our ways that we think we have life all figured out, that we are right on target in our thinking and in our beliefs. We think that we're never wrong and that it's always the other person who could use some changing for the better. If we ever do get to such a place in our lives, we must stop and realize that the person who needs to change the most is the one who looks at us every day in the mirror. We need to examine ourselves to find out where, in our own lives, we could change for the better.

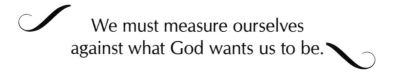

We must measure ourselves
against what God wants us to be.

The "mirror" that we need to look into for this purpose is the one that is spoken of in James 1:22–25. We must gaze into the *"perfect law of liberty"* (verse 25) and see ourselves measured against what God wants us to be. Obviously, being fallen humans, there are going to be areas in our lives that will need to be changed. We will need to change the ways we think so that we can have the *"mind of Christ"* (1 Cor. 2:16). This transformation will take time and effort, sometimes painful effort, as we choose to renew our minds each day and turn our backs on the worldly thoughts that try to dominate our minds. (See Romans 12:2.) The pain of such change is always worthwhile because the result is that we will become more like Christ and learn to think godly thoughts that glorify the Lord and keep us close to Him, which means we will stay in His plan for our lives.

We will also need to change the way we believe. This can be very painful to us. So often, we get to a place where we think we have this or that figured out theologically, even if we don't consciously think in those terms when we are actually in error. Maybe we heard a preacher say something we took for the truth without actually verifying it in the Scriptures. Then, one day down the road, we were challenged by what we read in the Bible to expand our belief in that particular area. It seemed to go against everything we had learned and thought we knew, but it was the truth. Or, maybe the preacher hadn't said anything in error, but we just took something he said and started to build our own theology out of it. When the day comes that we must change or modify a belief, it can be a painful process to expand our so-called theological box and make room for something new and different. But if we are to grow in our knowledge of God, it will mean growing in our understanding of Him and His Word. This, in turn, demands that we make room for change in our beliefs. No one is perfect in his theology because none of us is God. So, we are going to have to be flexible enough to go through the pain of change in our beliefs because, if we don't, we will find ourselves straying from the plan of God for our lives.

Another area that can be a painful change for us is that of our emotions. So many of us have emotions that need to just get kicked out the door. We probably don't think we do, but all of us could find some emotion within us that tends to get us into trouble. It could be our tempers. Think about how someone's temper will hurt not only him, but also all the people around him.

And I don't mean just physically. Uncontrolled anger can severely hurt those it is aimed against. It can cause scars that last a lifetime. An emotion like this can do nothing but keep us from walking fully toward our destinies because all it does is hinder our spiritual growth. It has to go. But it won't be easy. Getting rid of a dangerous emotion, whether it's a bad temper or raging jealousy, means we are going to have to change. We are going to have to make an effort to change our ways. We may even have to go through the pain of finding someone to help us with this change. But it's all worth it because it will make us more Christlike, which means we're going to keep growing spiritually and advancing toward that destined place God has called us to.

I don't think I even need to tell you that the thing we need to change the most is the sin we consciously live in. I know that uncontrolled thoughts, poor theology, and even bad emotions can all be considered sin. But I'm talking about those things we do in our lives that we know are without question sinful. These sins have to go, brothers and sisters. I know they can hold us in bondage, and I know they can have great power in our lives. It may seem as if you've dealt with the same sin for years. But deal with it again! Sin means we missed the mark spiritually, and if we keep on sinning, we are just going to erode the foundations of our faith. As it says in Proverbs 14:34, *"Sin is a reproach to any people."* If sin is allowed to remain in a person's life, you can believe that spiritual laziness and a backsliding spirit will soon follow. This means that the person will quickly fall by the wayside of God's destiny for his life.

Is getting rid of sin easy? Oh, it's easy to be forgiven of sin. Christ did all the work for our forgiveness when

He died on the cross. But getting rid of sin in our lives is another thing entirely. It will mean crucifying our flesh daily, choosing to live in holiness even when the mind or flesh is crying out for gratification. It will mean, perhaps, staying away from people we consider close to us, but who always seem to drag us down toward sin. It will sometimes mean seeking out someone to help us find our way out of the maze of sin. In other words, it will mean pain. But the pain is nothing compared to the glory that will be revealed in us as we find ourselves that much closer to our destiny!

In fact, we need to consider that remaining in our sin is going to bring us even more pain. Not only will it destroy us spiritually, but it can also very well destroy us physically or mentally. Additionally, it can inflict pain on those who are closely connected to us as well as others around us. It's just not worth it when you look at it from the viewpoint of staying on the path to destiny!

Another area of change that few people probably think about is that of altering our lives to stay in God's divine will. Obviously, we need to get rid of wrong thinking and sin in our lives if we are to abide in God's will. However, I'm talking about making a change in life when we know God is specifically telling us to do it. More often than not, this change will come to us as a part of His plan for our destiny. The only problem is that such a change will mean more pain in our lives, and we know it, too. That's why, so often, we choose to just avoid what God is calling us to do next. We are comfortable where we are, and we don't want to have to step out and face something new and different. This situation happened to me.

Destiny

When my mom died, my whole world came crashing down around me. It was a difficult time for me, and not just because I lost my mom. I realized my life was going to have to undergo a drastic change. I was twenty-one years old, and I had been living with my mom when she died. When I was under her roof, I knew she would take care of me, and she took care of a lot of the things in life that I should have already known how to do, such as managing my money and even paying the rent. I basically put off growing into manhood because I was in such a comfort zone living with my mom.

I should have been stretching myself to change and grow as a man all along because, after my mom died, I was suddenly forced to change into a man. My mom's death may have helped me become a man, but it was a painful process, probably more painful than it would have been if I had been changing my youthful ways all along. But God had me right where He wanted me after my mom's death. I was in a place where I still could have tried to remain in my comfort zone and get by the best I could. If I had done that, I would have quickly found my life spiraling out of control because of my lack of knowledge when it came to being responsible. Obviously, I didn't choose that path. I decided to grow into manhood and learn the things I needed to so that I could become a responsible adult. It was a big change for me, and it brought a lot of pain and suffering, but it was worth it.

Knowing God's will but choosing not to follow it is a very dangerous place to be in. It may seem as if life is easier if you just avoid it and stay in your little comfort zone. But let me tell you, the pain of changing and following God's plan each step of the way is a lot less severe than the pain we will experience if we try to run from God's will. Just ask Jonah. He refused to do the thing God commanded him to do, and he ended up in the belly of a whale.

I don't know about you, but I think I would rather make small, gradual changes when I have the opportunity and suffer that kind of pain instead of getting stuck having to make a wholesale change that brings incredible pain. Oh, there will be times when God asks us to make great changes in our lives, and they may very well bring with them intense pain. But if God has called us to walk that path, He will give us the grace and strength we need to overcome the pain and see our destinies unfold.

So, let's decide that, in spite of the pain that change causes in our own personal lives, we will do whatever it takes to grow closer to God and move toward our destinies.

Ships in the Night

Have you ever remembered someone you hadn't thought of for a long time? We all probably have. It's amazing to think about how many people we cross paths with in the span of our lives. People come, and people go, and we sometimes get the chance to know them in close relationship.

It is in those relationships that we must be ready to deal with the pain of change, because I can guarantee you that it will come. Think back to the story at the beginning of this chapter. The young man knew how much he liked the girl he was dating, and it was a painful struggle for him to let her go. But remember that letting her go moved him closer to his destiny in God. The same principle is true for us. We need to be ready to part with people in our lives no matter what the cost to us is.

I'm not saying that the partings will always take place because you realize that someone is not part of God's plan for your life. It may very well be that God has called a certain friend of yours to a new ministry, and he has to leave your area. Even a change like that can be painful because you will miss your friend's support and encouragement and just the ability to talk to him whenever you want.

Or, it could be that God has called you to pull up roots and move to another area. You will have to leave your friends, and possibly family, behind. It can be tough to leave the people closest to us.

> Life is all about change. The only
> thing that won't change is that
> there will always be change!

Or, the change could be the passing of a loved one. Losing someone to death is very painful. It is something we will all face, so we must be ready to deal with the pain, put it behind us, and not let it hinder us in our walk with God. Grief can easily get us offtrack in regard to our destinies. It's very common for Christians to lose heart and hope after seeing a family member or friend pass on. But we can't! If we are to seize all that God has planned for us, we must learn to expect and deal with the pain that comes with people exiting our lives.

Even people entering our lives can bring pain. There are individuals who just seem to rub us the wrong way. But do you think God is big enough to give us grace to go on when we experience relationships like that? Of course He is. It may very well be that the grating person you are in some sort of relationship with has been put in your life to help you walk in grace yourself, thus making you more Christlike in your attitude toward others.

So, let us remember that people are going to come into our lives, and people are going to leave us, as well. Many of these comings and goings will cause us pain. But we need to walk in the grace and mercy of God so that we can learn to recognize the pain these times cause us and then deal with the pain so we can move toward our destinies.

Master the Moment

The last major area of change we are going to look at is that of fluctuating situations and circumstances in our lives. No matter what we do to keep our lives consistent and unchanging, things around us are going to change. We may find that our company is going out of business and we will soon be without a job. We may be in a car accident and find that we just aren't able to do all the things we once could. Or, as we grow older, we may discover that our bodies and minds just aren't working the way they used to.

Of course, I could go on and on about possible changes in our lives. Life is all about change. In fact, the only thing that won't change in life is the fact that there will always be change! And, as we've already seen, change can bring pain, and lots of it. Therefore, we need to be ready to face the pain of changing situations and circumstances. It really comes down to us being able to roll with the punches that come our way in life.

Destiny

Let's take a look at the apostle Paul. Here was a man who was once a high-ranking Jew bent on destroying Christians. Then, on the way to Damascus, he had a life-changing experience that transformed him from being a persecutor of the church to being a believer. (See Acts 9:1–20.) Paul's life got even more interesting from then on. As Paul put it,

Five times I received from the Jews the forty lashes minus one. Three times I was beaten with rods, once I was stoned, three times I was shipwrecked, I spent a night and a day in the open sea, I have been constantly on the move. I have been in danger from rivers, in danger from bandits, in danger from my own countrymen, in danger from Gentiles; in danger in the city, in danger in the country, in danger at sea; and in danger from false brothers. I have labored and toiled and have often gone without sleep; I have known hunger and thirst and have often gone without food; I have been cold and naked. Besides everything else, I face daily the pressure of my concern for all the churches. (2 Cor. 11:24–28 NIV)

Obviously, becoming a believer and being filled with the Holy Ghost didn't exactly make Paul's life any easier. Although he was changed for the better, he still experienced pain. So, what was Paul's answer to the fluctuating situations he faced?

I have learned to be content whatever the circumstances. I know what it is to be in need, and I know what it is to have plenty. I have learned the secret of being content in any and every situation, whether well fed or hungry, whether living in [abundance or in need]. I can do everything through [Christ] who gives me strength. (Phil. 4:11–13 NIV)

That has to be our answer to the painful changes that come our way in life, no matter what the cause.

People will come and go. Situations and circumstances will change. We will face changes that need to be made in our own personal lives. No matter what the change is, there is only one response if we know God's will for our lives. We need to stay strong in faith and say, as Paul did, "I can do everything through Christ who gives me strength." Then, we will be able to deal with change and the pain it brings. And we will be able to keep pursuing our destinies with our whole hearts.

Four

Getting Over the Past

4
Getting Over the Past

But this one thing I do, forgetting those things which are behind, and reaching forth unto those things which are before, I press toward the mark for the prize of the high calling of God in Christ Jesus.
—Philippians 3:13–14

D id you ever know a driver who was constantly checking his rearview mirror? Such drivers always have their eyes fixed on what is behind them, worrying about what they have already passed and anxious about what might be creeping up on them. Usually, these people tend to swerve on the road in an erratic fashion because they aren't paying attention to where they are on the road or where they are heading. In other words, they're bad news for themselves and those around them.

Now, maybe you're not one of those "rearview mirror" drivers when you're behind the wheel of a car. But are you one when it comes to traveling along the road to your destiny? Are you someone who just can't seem to get the past out of your mind's eye? Does it haunt you to the point that you can't focus on the present or look forward to the future? Are there choices that you made that you wish you could do over again? Are there events you wish you could have prevented? Were things done to you that have left wounds that still burn with pain?

I'm sure most of us could answer yes to at least one of these questions. The fact of the matter is that we all have things from our pasts that hurt, that cause regret, or that make us say, "If only I would have done this or that." The problem is not so much that these things exist in our minds, but rather how we deal with them and how much we let them hinder us on our destined path.

Going in Reverse

While there are many different ways the past can cause pain for us, I believe they fall mainly into four main areas: mistakes we have made, regrets we have, things that have happened to us or around us, and self-pity. Every one of these is a danger when it comes to remaining on the path of destiny because each of them can distract us from our walks with God and our desire to persevere toward the places God has called us to.

The first area, mistakes of the past, deals with things we have done that we just can't get over—sins that hang over our heads with guilt and condemnation. We may feel sorry that we committed the sin, and we may even have confessed the sin and tried to experience God's forgiveness. But we just choose to keep on letting the sin affect our thoughts. We let the sin become this monster in our mind, and we let it sit there, and the enemy feeds us his line of guilt and condemnation. We feel ashamed and unworthy. We feel as if there is no way God could ever forgive what we did. We feel as if there is no way He could ever use us for His purposes again.

Sins we have committed may be the most dangerous area when it comes to dealing with the past because the enemy can use the shame of past sins as a sort of bondage. The shackles we choose to live in when we let past sin control our minds will first slow us down on our destined journey and then finally force us to fall by the wayside, rendering us ineffective and unproductive in our walk with God.

Along the same lines is the area of regret. Dwelling on sin from the past is thinking about what we've already done. Living in regret is thinking about what we never did or accomplished. Regret is almost as deadly as letting past sin enslave us because it will always keep our focus on what we could have done instead of what we should be doing now. This is the classic "If only" syndrome: "If only I had gone to college." "If only I had taken that new job." "If only I had married that person." "If only I had shown more love to my family."

Regret is a dangerous trap because there is no way we can fully focus our mind and spirit on the day at hand if we dwell on what should or could have been. It is an area that affects many people and keeps them from what God wants to do in their lives now and in the future. Regret, like past sin, can bind us on our journeys to destiny if we let it dominate our minds.

Another area from the past that can distract and detour us from our destinies is made up of things that happened to us or around us. It might be a variety of things that took place in days gone by. It could be the death of a loved one. It could be a derogatory comment from a father or mother when we were very young. It could even be something like losing a scholarship to someone else in high school. Whatever it might be, it is an event that in some way affected us then and is still affecting our lives today.

Again, this area of the past can distract us from our destinies if we allow the pain of the event to continue to hurt us each day. Such painful occurrences in life can bind us by forcing us to live our lives in hurt or terror or anxiety or anger and bitterness. We may begin to think that God failed us when He let these things happen. In this way, a wall goes up between us and God, a wall of our own construction. The wall, of course, will prevent us from walking in close fellowship with God and, in turn, cause us to quickly get off our path to destiny.

The last area of the past that can distract us from our destinies is self-pity. We will have to learn to deal with this area if we want to achieve all that God has called us to do in this life. Self-pity is such a common thing in people. How many times do we hear others, or even ourselves, saying, "Poor me! Look at how bad I've had it in my life! Everyone else has it so good, but not me!"

Sound familiar? I'm sure it does, whether it was coming into your ears or out of your own mouth. For some reason, we have this notion that the world revolves around us and that, if we're not happy, then something's wrong. It's as if we think God falls off His throne when it comes to handling the things we've gone through in the past. We sit in our little pity party, feeling sorry for ourselves. Of course, we're the only ones who attend this party because who wants to be around someone who is singing the "Woe Is Me" song?

Self-pity restricts our view of our destinies by keeping our focus on "poor little ole me" instead of on the calling of God in our lives. We get into a rut that sometimes makes us think things were always better in the past. It's just like when the children of Israel were wandering around in the desert after leaving Egypt. Even though they had been freed from their oppressive slavery, they actually began to complain and say that they wanted to go back to the good old days of Egypt! This is something that a lot of us go through, but we will have to find our way out of such an attitude if we are ever to walk in the fullness of God's plan for our lives.

All these areas of the past are ways the enemy can detour us from our destinies if we are not careful. Satan will take every opportunity to keep bringing the past back to our remembrance. It's a tool of the enemy that can seriously hurt us, and it is something that the devil knows we have trouble dealing with. His darts sting and are painful, and, eventually, they will take us down if we let them, preventing us from living out our destinies.

Getting over the Hump

So, what is the answer to dealing with the pain of the past in our lives? I've seen many people come through battles with their pasts. Some of them have won the battles, while others have succumbed to the pain and fallen away from God and their destinies. Getting over the past is no easy thing, as you probably already know. In my own life, I've had to deal with the past more than a few times.

I remember the day my mom passed away. It was a Sunday morning, and my mother and I were at home getting ready for church. Because she had to help out at church that day, we were supposed to get there a little early. I remember I was just dragging around the house, and she didn't want to leave without me. She kept saying, "Hurry up!" Finally, I got dressed and called out to her, "Okay, I'm ready!" I didn't get a response, so I went to check on her. I found her slumped in a chair, dead from a heart attack.

Now, obviously, this was a traumatic event for me. But I let it latch on to my life to the degree that I wouldn't let go of it. I let this past event begin to control my life. I kept going to church, but I wasn't interested in it. I kept reading the Bible, but I was lazy in my walk with God. Eventually, I started to fall into self-pity, saying things like, "It's not fair! Why did she have to go? Why, God?" I was just so sad to see her go. I let her death haunt me for almost a year.

Finally, one day, I was sitting in a deep state of loneliness when I heard the Holy Spirit ask me, "Are you going to let this kill you, or do you want to live?" Right then, I said, "I want to live." And that's what I did. I began to live in the now again. I began to take charge of my life by the grace of God and His strength. As I wrote earlier, it turned out that my mom's death helped propel me into manhood. Until that point, I had become very dependent on her for many of the basic things in my life. Having her taken from me forced me to grow up and take responsibility for myself. Even though I did grow spiritually lazy following my mom's death, I never lost sight of the destiny for my life. I hung on to the vision I had when I was a little boy, and it carried me through the pain to the point where God could finally get me over the hump of the past.

Not only did finally getting over my mother's death make me grow up into manhood, but it also set into motion the strength to go after the vision I had as a little boy that landed me on the stage of Radio City Music Hall. The day I told the Holy Spirit that I wanted to live, I sat down and wrote my first song, called "I'll Make It." It was an anthem of what I had been through. It was a song of how God had lifted me up out of the pit of despair. I recorded that song with the Love Fellowship Choir in 1985, and it landed us on the top of the gospel music charts. Out of the pain of my mother's death came new life in the form of my destiny taking shape. But it took a determined decision on my part that I would not let my past defeat me. I knew I had to go out and get my destiny, and I finally did it.

No matter how the past may be haunting us, we must learn to overcome the pain and anguish if we are ever to get on with our journey toward destiny.

Are you trapped by the weight of past sin in your life? Then, stand up and begin to believe in the forgiveness of God. Believe that He removed our sins from us as far as the east is from the west (Ps. 103:12). Believe that, if we confess our sins to Him, He will forgive our sins and the blood of Jesus His Son will cleanse us from all unrighteousness (1 John 1:9). We must change our attitude toward past sin and learn to walk in the forgiveness God has given us through the Cross of Christ.

If it's a matter of a recurring sin in your life, something that started years ago, then you must take drastic measures. Addictions or sinful habits are absolute back-breakers when it comes to staying on the path of destiny. You just can't have it both ways. Either you're living for God and what He has planned for your life, or else you're dwelling in darkness with no hope for the future or even the present. Do what it takes to beat the sin. Pray, read the Bible, meditate on the Word. Surround yourself with people who will hold you accountable and keep your focus on God. Renounce the sin in your life. Flee from it when it comes back to tempt you yet again. Seek out help, if it comes to that, and talk to someone who can give you a plan to beat the sin that continues to haunt you and suck you in. Dear brothers

> You can't have it both ways.
> Either you're living for God, or
> you're dwelling in darkness.

and sisters, this has to be done if we are to walk in the plans God has for our lives! So, get over the sin, and get on with your destiny!

How about those of you who have a lot of regrets in your life? Start meditating on the truth of the verse that says, *"All things work together for good to them that love God"* (Rom. 8:28). The things you regret are water under the bridge, in God's eyes. Those choices you made so long ago that still haunt your mind? They are done with. They are impossible to do over. Get in the here and now, and don't make the same mistake again of not doing something you know you should do. But don't get hung up if you fall short again when it comes to making a decision or living up to what you know you should be. We have to know that God is big enough to order our steps even when we think we might have messed them up by not seizing the moment at some point in our lives.

What about allowing events of the past to control us? We need to start remembering that the past is just what it is: the past. Maybe the events did cause us trauma or bitterness or fear or anger. Whatever they caused, we need to remember that God has given us a spirit of power, love, and a sound mind (2 Tim. 1:7). The emotions that past events are causing in our lives today have to go. I now live by that principle. We all need to believe that God can give us a peace that passes all understanding (Phil. 4:7) and that we have the mind of Christ (1 Cor. 2:16), a mind that can help us overcome the events of the past and live for today.

When it comes to past events controlling our lives, I can't help but think of a young man I ministered to at our church in Brooklyn some time ago. He told me the tragic tale of how his uncle had sexually abused him as a child. The young man felt the shame and bitterness of the event as he was growing up, and he let it infect his mind with rage and anger and an uncontrollable hatred. It got to where he really didn't understand what it was to love or to be loved, so he began looking for love in all the wrong places.

Somehow, by the grace of God, this young man came to our church one day, and at the end of the service, I felt prompted to give an altar call for anyone who had been abused in any way in their lives. I opened up the altar and asked people to come down for prayer about the abuse in their lives. The young man got into a line that stretched all the way to the back of the church. When he finally reached the altar, he told me he just couldn't get away from that time so long ago when his uncle hurt him so badly. It was an event that dominated his mind and influenced everything he did.

After our initial meeting at the altar, I began to sit and talk with the man in counseling. Little by little, we broke down the walls of the past through prayer and talking about how to build a strong foundation in life based on a relationship with God. The thing that helped him the most was the Lord convicting him about denying the past. He sensed God was telling him to go back to the past and deal with it, instead of denying it and letting it run his life. The man decided to go back in his mind to confront this painful event from his past. He understood that the only way to his freedom was to kill what was binding him from the root. After many sessions together, the man finally broke through and took hold of what I had been telling him. Today, he is over the hump of the past, and he is walking in God's destiny for his life.

The final area of the past that must be dealt with is that of the self-pity that creeps into our lives and dominates our thinking. First of all, it's time for us to remember that this world does not revolve around us. It revolves around the Lord and Savior of our lives, Jesus Christ. Also, we need to start asking ourselves, "Who do you think you are?" In other words, what right do we have to mope and complain about what happened to us in the past? We really need to stop and get a bird's-eye view of our situation in life. If we do that, we will probably see that our self-pity is totally unjustified because what happened to us in the past is so small in the grand scheme of things. Is that thing of your past so powerful that it should affect today and the future? Absolutely not! It's time to kick self-pity out of our lives and to remember that *"in Him we live and move and have our being"* (Acts 17:28 NKJV).

Under the Blood

If there is one thing that we can do more than anything else to help us conquer the pain of the past in our lives, it is to always remember that everything that happened "back then" is now under the blood of Jesus. Sins, regrets, haunting events, the things that cause self-pity—they're all under the blood. As born-again believers, we are cleansed from our sins and given a new heart, a new spirit. The old things have passed away, and everything has become new in our lives (2 Cor. 5:17). We need to learn to walk in the newness of life that Christ has given us.

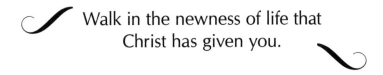

> Walk in the newness of life that
> Christ has given you.

It's not enough to just say there's nothing we can do about the pain of the past. We need to get over it and get on with it. If you've seen your destined place in God or if you're just living for today's destiny, you must take the past by the throat and put it where it belongs: in the past. To be sure, there are things we can learn from the past. Everything that has happened to us has helped make us who we are today. But let's not get caught up in the past, not even the good things of the days gone by. We can just as easily get stuck wishing for the "good old days" as we can being controlled by the pain of the past. Brothers and sisters, these *are* the good old days. We're living in them right now. So, let's learn from the past and appreciate the good things God has brought our way. Let's rejoice that the pain of the past has helped us mature in Christ. But let's leave the past in the past and go forward to our destinies in God!

Five

Seize the Moment

5
Seize the Moment

Not that I have already attained, or am already
perfected; but I press on, that I may lay hold of that
for which Christ Jesus has also laid hold of me.
—Philippians 3:12 (NKJV)

D id you ever hear the story from the Bible of the four lepers who helped save the city of Samaria? Being lepers, these four men were forever cast out of society, destined to live out their days in solitude with other lepers outside the city. (See Leviticus 13:45–46.)

During the time of a great invasion by the Syrian army, the lepers were sitting at the entrance to the city gate, considering what they should do.

"Well, we could try to get back into the city," one of the men said.

"Nah, we'd just end up starving like everyone else because of the Syrian siege out there," another replied.

"Well," the third said, "we could just sit here and die."

"Forget it!" said the last one. "Let's just head over to the Syrians. If they kill us, we'll be as dead as we would if we keep sitting here. If they don't kill us, then we'll live and have food!"

"Let's do it," the others replied.

So, they went up to the Syrian encampment. But when they got there, they were surprised at what they found. All the tents were there, but no one was to be seen. The lepers didn't know it, but God had scared every one of those Syrian soldiers right out of their beds the night before. Now, the lepers were standing in the midst of all the wealth of the Syrians. Let me tell you, it was like Christmas for the lepers in that camp. They ran into the tents and ate all the food and drink they wanted. Then, they took gold, silver, and clothing from the tents and hid it. Finally, one of them looked at the others and shook his head.

"Guys, we ain't being nothing but selfish!" he said. "Come on! Let's go to the city and tell the people about this."

They all agreed. So, they went off to the city. They sent a message to the king telling him of the good fortune that had presented itself. But the king didn't believe it, thinking instead it was a trap laid by the Syrians. Finally, one of the king's servants sent a group of men to the camp to see if the story of the lepers was true. Soon enough, the group of men was on its way back to the city with the good news. Samaria had a party that night, let me tell you. And it was all thanks to four lepers who grabbed life by the horns right then and there. They didn't linger in the city, the place of their past where nothing but death awaited them. They got up and seized the moment. It's a lesson we all need to learn if we are to achieve our destinies in life. (See 2 Kings 7:1–16.)

The Matter at Hand

Too often, we as Christians are preoccupied by either the past or the future. We like to bask in the glory of past experiences, or else we get stuck in dealing with pain from long ago. We sit and long for the future, waiting to see what God is going to do in our lives, or else we fret over what might be around the corner. We're either in the rut of rewind or fast-forward. What's the solution? That's right, we have to hit the play button and live right now. Our destinies aren't accomplished either by dreaming about the past or worrying about it, and they're not fulfilled by fantasizing about or fearing the future. Destiny is lived in the here and now. We would be wise to understand that the steps we take on our

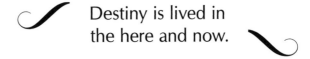

Destiny is lived in the here and now.

destined paths build off the past and carry us to the future. But they are still steps that have to be taken now.

How can we expect to be useful in God's purposes for our lives if we are only concerned about the past or the future? As the saying goes, "Learn from the past, look forward to the future, but live for today!" I think that statement sums up what our goal should always be as we strive toward our destinies. "Be here now" is another way of saying it. The point is the same: We need to seize the moment and not worry about the past or the future.

Prepare for the Present

There are some things that we can all do to stay on our paths of destiny and be effective in our call each day. These things are the basic training of Christianity, so to speak. In Christianity, the training never ends because it's the basics that strengthen our faith.

- **Prayer:** Prayer seems to be an area of great confusion in the church today. People can't seem to figure out such questions as, "When should I pray?" "What do I say?" "How do I know God is listening?" We need to quit making excuses and just pray! Prayer is coming before God and spending time with Him, fellowshipping with the Father and enjoying His presence. Prayer, ultimately, can be broken down into two areas: relational and request. Relational prayer is the time we spend building our relationships with God, just spending time loving Him and receiving His love. Request prayer is, of course, the things we bring before God as the needs of our hearts. In any case, prayer can be something that we need to learn discipline to do. Paul said to *"persevere in prayer"* (Rom. 12:12 NRSV). This may not be easy, especially at first, but as we grow in our relationships with God, we will find ourselves excited about the chance to pray. Prayer is something that keeps us sensitive to God's will for our lives and helps us stay on the path to our destinies.

- **Reading the Word:** What happens when you squeeze a wet sponge? Everything that is in it comes running out, right? So it is with our lives. When trials and suffering come, we will show what's inside us. Hopefully, our words and actions will show that we have immersed ourselves in Scripture and that we are hiding His Word in our hearts. His words can give us strength for today and hope for the future. But it is up to us to read the Word every day. We must be studying the Scriptures and applying them to our lives daily. This will help us in our understanding of God and His plan for our lives.

- **Praise and worship:** Praise and worship goes hand in hand with prayer. When we praise and worship God, we enter into His presence, where the only thing that matters is Him. Praise will carry us through difficult times by keeping our focus on God's magnificent love and grace. Worshipping Him when things are going smoothly keeps us close to Him and in His will for us. We can bask in His glory and find strength and power for every situation while on the journey He has called us to.

- **Spiritual warfare:** Prayer, praise, and reading the Word are all forms of spiritual warfare. By being faithful in these areas, we can, of course, be strong spiritually and fight off the attacks of the enemy that will inevitably come. You can bet that the devil will always be hanging around, looking for an opportunity to derail us from our destined paths. That's why we need to be serious about spiritual warfare. We need to put on the belt of truth so that the truth of God's Word will hold our lives together, no matter what we hear or see. We need to put on the breastplate of righteousness so that we can keep our hearts pure before God. We need to fit our feet with the readiness that comes from the powerful Gospel of peace. We need to take up the shield of faith that will protect us from the enemy's attacks as we stand strong in our belief in God. We need to have on the helmet of salvation so that we can keep our thoughts holy. Finally, we need to take up the sword of the Spirit, which is the Word of God, so that we can stand on the Word in every situation. (See Ephesians 6:10–18.)

- **Fruit of the Spirit:** Many people may not think about the fruit of the Spirit in regard to staying strong in God and on their paths to destiny. But if we would begin to dwell and meditate on the fruit of the Spirit mentioned in Galatians 5:22–23, we would find ourselves becoming more and more like Christ, which means we would be walking more closely with Him and His will for our lives. Think about it: love, joy, peace, longsuffering, gentleness, goodness, faith, meekness, temperance. All of us could use more of these qualities in our lives. If we take the time to meditate on these traits, we will start to see ourselves and others in a different light. We will start to walk in the fruit of the Spirit, and we will find ourselves closer to God and to our destiny.

- **Fellowship with the body of Christ:** One thing I think we forget sometimes when it comes to walking this path of destiny is that none of us are in this thing alone. We are part of the body of Christ. As Paul put it, we are the *"temple of God"* (1 Cor. 3:16) and *"one body in Christ, and individually members of one another"* (Rom. 12:5 NKJV). We are all part of God's grand plan for the perpetuation of His kingdom here on earth. This means that the destinies of us all are intertwined in the corporate destiny of the church. This, in turn, means that we need to have the attitude of teammates when it comes to accomplishing our individual destinies as part of the church's corporate destiny. We all have a part to play. We need to use the gifts God has given us to fulfill our own destinies and the destiny of the church. We can't think about ourselves as loners and take the attitude of "me against the world." Instead, we all have to be diligent in our individual call within the corporate destiny. As Paul said in 1 Corinthians 12:15–22 (NIV),

If the foot should say, "Because I am not a hand, I do not belong to the body," it would not for that reason cease to be part of the body. And if the ear should say, "Because I am not an eye, I do not belong to the body," it would not for that reason cease to be part of the body. If the whole body were an eye, where would the sense of hearing be? If the whole body were an ear, where would the sense of smell be? But in fact God has arranged the parts in the body, every one of them, just as he wanted them to be. If they were all one part, where would the body be? As it is, there are many parts, but one body. The eye cannot say to the hand, "I don't need you!" And the head cannot say to the feet, "I don't need you!" On the contrary, those parts of the body that seem to be weaker are indispensable.

We must realize that one person's individual destiny is no more or less important than the next person's because we are all part of the grand plan of God. Therefore, we must not forsake the *"assembling of ourselves"* as a church body (Heb. 10:25). We need to be around other Christians to understand what God wants us to do as a body. We also need to be around other Christians so that we can build each other up in the Lord and be there for one another in times of need. As it says in Ecclesiastes 4:9–10 (NKJV),

Two are better than one, because they have a good reward for their labor. For if they fall, one will lift up his companion. But woe to him who is alone when he falls, for he has no one to help him up.

So, let's keep in mind the corporate destiny of the church and how our individual destinies are a part of it. Let's not forget that we need each other in our walk with Christ.

Pathway to the Future

When we seize the moment in the present, we do all we can to achieve our destinies in the now. It's like

Other Christians can build us up and be there in times of need.

building a brick wall. A bricklayer doesn't just go right to laying the top row of bricks so that he can call the project done. No, he has to lay one brick on the other. Then, after every brick is in place, they form a completed wall. It's the same in our Christian walk toward destiny. If we think of our destiny as the completed wall, then we realize we need to stay faithful each day to "lay the bricks" that will bring us to our fulfilled destiny.

Think of what Paul meant when he said,

Brethren, I count not myself to have apprehended: but this one thing I do, forgetting those things which are behind, and reaching forth unto those things which are before, I press toward the mark for the prize of the high calling of God in Christ Jesus. (Phil. 3:13–14)

Not only did he say he was forgetting the past and reaching to the future, but he also said he was pressing on toward the mark. In other words, he was doing what he could in the *now* to lay hold of that for which Christ laid hold of him when He set him on the path of destiny (verse 12).

Faith for the future is a wonderful thing. We can dream about the future and all it holds for us. We can say that we are stepping out in faith to see something we expect God to do in the future. But what about having faith for the now? If we are going to take hold of our destinies, we need to have faith to surrender to God now! For without faith, it is absolutely impossible to please Him (Heb. 11:6). And if we are not pleasing Him in the now, we are not abiding in Him and His will for our lives.

I am a firm believer in taking advantage of opportunity. There's a place in God that you can reach where He will open the doors of opportunity for you. At one point in my own life, the door of opportunity was open so wide that I couldn't even believe that the thing I had been praying for was right there in front of me! The Lord allowed me to see the things I had hoped for; but, more importantly, He showed me that I could have them now. It makes me think of Hebrews 11:1: *"Now faith is the substance of things hoped for, the evidence of things not seen."* I understand that this Scripture is talking about what faith is, but I also like to think of the first two words—*"Now faith."* It's faith in the now that is needed!

So, remember, there is nothing wrong with looking ahead to the future or even thinking back to where we once were in life. But it is in the now that we will take the steps that lead to the fulfillment of our destinies.

Samson in the Now

Even though Samson often found himself in many predicaments because of his sinful ways, it is still interesting to note how many times he took advantage of the chances God gave him in his life.

After marrying a Philistine woman against the wishes of his parents and, no doubt, God, Samson found out that his bride had betrayed him by giving her people the answer to a riddle he had given them to solve. The reward for answering the riddle correctly was to be thirty linen garments and thirty sets of clothes. So, after Samson heard the Philistines give the correct answer to the riddle, and after making his wife's treachery known to all, he got up to fetch the promised prize. He went out, found thirty other Philistines and killed them. Then he took their clothes and offered them to those who had answered his riddle correctly. Samson made the most of a bad situation and seized the moment, helping to rid the land of the Philistines.

When he returned to his Philistine wife and found out that her father had given her away to someone else, thinking that Samson wanted nothing to do with her after her betrayal of him, Samson, just a bit peeved by the whole situation, stalked out into the fields and caught three hundred foxes, no small feat. He tied the foxes together by their tails in pairs and then attached a burning torch to each pair. He then sent the foxes running through the Philistines' fields and watched as their crops quickly went up into flames. Again, Samson took advantage of the opportunity that presented itself, and he wreaked havoc once more on Israel's oppressor.

But seeing their fields on fire didn't exactly thrill the Philistines. They banded together and went after Samson. Most of them met with a gruesome end at the hands of God's warrior-judge as Samson once more seized the moment and fought with a fury in the now.

Destiny

Tired of fighting the Philistines, Samson went into hiding, only to be discovered by some men from Judah. These men told Samson that he was making life tough for the rest of Israel and that the Philistines were making camp nearby in an attempt to capture him. Samson agreed to give himself over to the Philistines to appease the men from Judah. When Samson, bound in ropes by the men of Judah, came upon the Philistines, he snapped the ropes and roared as he lunged toward the enemy. Seeing the jawbone of a donkey lying on the ground nearby, he grabbed it and began using it to batter the Philistines. Samson stopped swinging the jawbone after slaying a thousand of the heathen troops, again doing the most with the day at hand.

Then came Samson's greatest and most tragic case of seizing the moment. After being tricked by the Philistine Delilah, Samson was captured by the enemy army. His eyes were gouged out, and he was hauled away to the city of Gaza. There, the mighty champion of God was forced into manual labor in the Philistine prison. Eventually, the Philistines took Samson out of prison to make sport of him in their temple. The giant building was brimming with joyous Philistines, all of whom were thrilled to see their greatest foe finally beaten down and defeated. Standing in the temple without sight, Samson again seized the moment. He told the servant who was guiding him to let him lean on the pillars of the temple. As soon as Samson felt the stone pillars with his hands, he roared, "Let me die with the Philistines!" And then he pushed with all his might against the giant columns until they fell over and crumbled. Three thousand Philistines died that day along with Samson, who understood better than most that opportunities such as he had are rare and must be seized or forever lost. (See Judges 14:12–15:17; 16:4–30.)

Now, obviously, Samson lived in a different day and age than we do. He resorted to force and violence as a means to seize the moment. But we can still learn a valuable lesson from the mighty man of God. Every chance he had to take care of business in his life, he took. Every chance he had to take back ground from the enemy, he took. And even when the odds were against him doing anything else of value in this life, he used the resources at hand to accomplish God's purposes.

That's the kind of attitude I'm talking about here! We need to take back everything the enemy has stolen from us. We need to be on the lookout for chances to serve God with all our hearts in the day-after-day drudgery of life. We need to be sensitive to the Holy Ghost when He is giving us the chance to do something worthwhile. Do you see someone hurting today? Go and pray for him. Do you see someone who could use a helping hand? Offer him one. Do you see a neighbor who needs some comfort in life? Share the Gospel with him. Do you see a little child who is hungry and without clothes? Provide for his needs.

Whatever you do, do something now! An old saying goes, "Find a need and fill it." That's what this life is all about. We find needs in our own lives and the lives of others. Let's do all we can to recognize these needs and then fill them right now!

Six

Hope for the Future

6
Hope for the Future

*For I know the thoughts that I think toward you, says
the LORD, thoughts of peace and not of evil, to give
you a future and a hope.*
—Jeremiah 29:11 (NKJV)

I once heard the story of a brilliant man, which still brings tears to my eyes. This man was born in the South. He had a rough childhood, with very little to call his own. But he had within himself a drive to rise above the poverty he lived in. So, when the other little boys were playing, he was studying or running errands for the folks in the neighborhood to make extra money for his family. As he grew a little older, he dreamed of becoming a musician because he loved the way the church musician played the organ for worship. Every Sunday after church, he would spend hours with the minister of music until he learned to play almost as well as his mentor did. Soon, the little boy became a young man and graduated from high school. All his hard work paid off as he earned a music scholarship to a nearby university. He completed his undergraduate work in three years and graduated with honors. Taking advantage of a graduate scholarship that the university offered to him, he breezed through his graduate courses, and he earned a doctorate in music studies.

The young man felt that he should give back to the university that had given him so much. So, he became a professor there, and he taught others who had a passion to learn about music. A year went by, and the professor found himself falling in love with the new secretary in the music department. Soon, the two were dating, and a year later, they were married. The man was in bliss, and he often thought back to those days when his parents could barely put food on his plate. Now, here he was a university professor, able to earn a good income and send his parents money each month. He had a nice home and a beautiful wife. He smiled when he thought about it all, and he knew without a doubt that dreams could come true.

Then, one day, his dream life became a nightmare. He had finished teaching a class in the morning and had rushed out to the department offices to see his wife, who was still working as a secretary at the school. Hoping to catch her before she went to lunch, the man was shocked to walk through the office doors and find a team of paramedics lifting his wife onto a stretcher. The professor ran to his wife, who lay motionless. Another female secretary, who was in tears, grabbed the professor by the arm and told him she was just coming to get him from class.

"What happened?" the professor asked as he clutched his wife's hand.

"They think it was a heart attack," the secretary told him.

The professor looked at his wife and then at the paramedics.

"How is she?" he asked.

"Sir, we lost her," a paramedic replied.

"Noooo!" the professor wailed. "Oh, my God, no!"

The professor fell to his knees, sobbing.

From that day on, the students noticed a difference in the professor. He was less jovial and more aloof with them. Then, a year later, the professor received the news that his mother had died. Several students who attended the same church as the professor noticed he hadn't attended for weeks after his mother's death.

In class, the professor became more and more despondent until the head of the music department finally called him into her office one day.

"Professor, I know it's been rough the past couple of years," the head of the department said. "But we need you to be here for your students. Several of them are concerned for you, and they've noticed quite a difference in your—well—in your personality in the classroom. It's almost as if you don't care anymore, they said."

The professor blew out a long breath and then rubbed his temples. He looked up at the head of the department with sullen eyes.

"Ma'am, you're absolutely right," he said as he rose from his chair. "I don't care anymore. I don't care about anything or anyone. I quit caring the day God quit caring about me. He robbed me of my future."

The professor turned to leave, then paused as he opened the door.

"There just isn't any hope left in my life," he whispered and then walked out the door.

Ten years later, in the city where the professor had taught, a youth choir from New York came to the area to do a concert. One of their stops took them to a soup kitchen where workers served breakfast to homeless men and women each morning. The choir and their director pitched right in, serving the men and women. Afterward, the choir director asked if anyone would like to sing a few songs before they left for the day. Several men and women muttered that they would very much like to. Then, the director asked if anyone would be kind enough to come up and play the old piano sitting in the corner while he led everyone in song.

A tall man with distinguished features stood up and walked to the piano. His clothes were tattered, and he looked painfully thin. The choir director smiled at the man as he took a seat at the piano and began to play. The director began singing, but he couldn't take his eyes off the man playing the piano.

The choir director looked into the man's eyes. Pain just seemed to resonate from them as he played and looked toward heaven. The director kept singing, but he could not stop thinking about the man. He wondered how someone who could play the piano like that could ever end up homeless on the streets.

As the choir director continued to sing, the pianist held back tears as he played and thought about the days of long ago when he was a professor and had a wife who loved him and there was hope for the future.

There Is Hope

That's a sad story, for sure, but I would guess that many Christians feel the very same way that the former professor did because of circumstances they have gone through. I don't know if there is anything worse than being in a state of absolute and utter hopelessness. There are many things in life that we have already discussed that can really slow us down on our journeys to destiny. But hopelessness can be totally devastating. It's something that sucks the life right out of us and keeps us in a place of complete inactivity. We feel as though the future holds nothing for us, and we think, "Why bother?"

Now, hopelessness can begin to creep into our lives through a tragedy, as in the case of the professor. When something like that happens, it can throw us into a tailspin that ends with a crash into despair if we are not careful to guard our hearts. Hopelessness can also begin with just the fearful thought of facing the future. In that case, it continues to build within us little by little as we sink into the depths of despair.

For whatever reason we may have fallen into a state of hopelessness, we need to remember that we can indeed have hope for the future. God promised it to us in Jeremiah 29:11, which says, *"For I know the thoughts that I think toward you, says the LORD, thoughts of peace and not of evil, to give you a future and a hope"* (NKJV). These words were spoken through the prophet Jeremiah to a group of Jewish exiles that had been deported from the land of Judah to Babylon by King Nebuchadnezzar. The exiles were no doubt aware that Jerusalem was about to fall to the Babylonians, which meant the end of Israel's inhabitation of the Promised Land. So, the Lord sent the exiles a message through Jeremiah to encourage them not to lose hope, even though the situation at hand seemed hopeless.

We need to remember that God has also promised us hope for the future no matter how hopeless things may seem to us. God has promised never to leave or forsake us (Josh. 1:5 NKJV). He is present to give us hope in even the most hopeless of circumstances. Paul emphasized faith, hope, and love, showing us the importance of keeping hope in our lives (1 Cor. 13:13 NKJV). In Romans 5:5, Paul also said that hope will not disappoint us *"because the love of God has been poured out in our hearts by the Holy Spirit who was given to us"* (NKJV). God's love is always more than enough to carry us through any hopelessness that comes our way. But we need to abide in God's will for our lives so that His Holy Ghost can strengthen us with hope for the future.

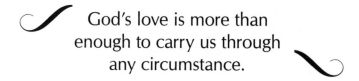

God's love is more than enough to carry us through any circumstance.

Reach for the Stars, but Keep Your Feet on the Ground

Knowing that we do, indeed, have a hope for the future, we can look expectantly in that direction. But as we discussed in the last chapter, we can't get so caught up in the future that we forget to live in the present. We need to keep ourselves grounded in the *now* while we look with hope to what God has planned for us for the future. As we remember what we have learned in the past and what we are to be doing right now, we can keep a healthy view of the future in mind.

Destiny

Think about Joshua, whose life we looked at a few chapters ago. Joshua came out of captivity in Egypt with the rest of the Israelites. Like them, he knew that God had promised the nation of Israel a land of its own, a land *"flowing with milk and honey"* (Exod. 13:5). Because he was one of the twelve spies whom Moses sent to search out the Promised Land, he saw the goodness of that land. The problem was that only he and Caleb thought that the Israelites, with God's help, could conquer it. The other ten spies were too scared of the "giants" who lived there, and they persuaded the rest of the Israelites not to go up into the land unless they wanted to be destroyed.

Talk about being on the edge of receiving the blessing of God! That's where Joshua was. He had heard God's promise to bring the Hebrews into the Promised Land. He had even seen how wonderful a land it would be to live in. He had the faith in God to know that the land could be theirs without question. He was probably champing at the bit to go right back to the Promised Land and take what he knew belonged to the Israelites based on God's promise. Then, all of a sudden, Joshua heard that the rest of the Israelites didn't want to go up and take the land. They were too scared. They didn't have enough faith. Let me tell you, Joshua was irate! He and Caleb both tore their clothes and pleaded with their fellow Israelites to trust God and watch Him bring His promise to pass. Yet, the Israelites would have none of it. They picked up stones to kill Joshua and Caleb, but God intervened to save them. The Lord appeared before all Israel and said that the Israelites would have to wait forty years before they could enter the Promised Land and that no one who was over twenty years old would see it because they hadn't trusted Him. Of course, that didn't include Joshua or Caleb, whom the Lord said would indeed enter the Promised Land. (See Numbers 13–14.)

Wow! Joshua must have just stood there with his jaw hanging open. Forty years he would have to wait! He was so close, and now he had to wander around in the desert until all the unbelievers died off. He wouldn't exactly be a young man by the time they finally got to conquer the Promised Land. But Joshua was smart enough to surrender his life to God. He knew his destiny was to live in the Promised Land. He kept in mind God's past promise, and he remembered the mighty acts of the Lord from his days in Egypt. He let his past buoy his faith in God. At the same time, he must have kept an eye on his future every day for those forty years. He knew how awesome the Promised Land was, and he no doubt smacked his parched lips in the desert sun when he thought of the fruit of the land that he would eventually call home. What a future to look forward to!

But Joshua didn't go floating along on his dream of the future for those forty years. As we saw in the second chapter of this book, Joshua stayed grounded in the present by serving the Lord right where he was. He continued to act as Moses' assistant and was given authority to help rule the people. (See Numbers 27:18–23.) Finally, when it was time for Moses to depart the earth, God declared that Joshua would lead the children of Israel into the Promised Land. What a turn of events! Joshua, who had been so close to living in the Promised Land forty years before, would now be God's chosen leader to lead the people into the land to conquer it!

Destiny

This is what I'm talking about—living with an expectant hope of the future, yet staying grounded in the present with a healthy view of the past in mind. We could talk about David, as well. As a young shepherd boy, he was anointed by Samuel to be king of the land. What a future to look forward to! But it would be years before David even came close to taking the throne. He had to avoid King Saul's repeated attempts to kill him. He had to flee into the land of the Philistines—Israel's hated enemies—to finally escape the wrath of Saul. He had to endure battle after battle and many heartaches along the way. But he knew what God had accomplished in his past, how the Lord had blessed him and protected him every step of the way. And he knew his destiny was to lead Israel as its king. The throne was his, and, by faith, he knew it would come to him.

But David didn't sit around in the woods waiting for Saul to die of old age. He did all he could in the "now" to help his destiny come to pass. All the time he spent as a fugitive warrior helped hone his battle skills and also earned him a good reputation with the people of Israel. When Saul finally did die and it was time for David to be king, he was ready. He had come forth through his trials as gold, and he was prepared to continue in his destiny as the ruler of Israel.

Just like Joshua, David looked forward with hope to the future, but he never forgot the past and he never avoided seizing the moment at hand. We need to learn this same lesson as we do all we can to go out and take hold of our destiny. We need to have a faith and a hope for the future without forgetting the lessons of the past or neglecting to take advantage of the now.

Better Things to Come

This lesson may seem all well and good to some of you. But, for others, it's not so easy to digest. You might be sitting there saying, "That's all great! But what if there is no hope for my future? All I've ever had in my life is pain, and I can't see it getting any better!"

If this is your situation, all I can say is, yes, it will get better. God hasn't fallen off the throne, and He knows your hurt and pain. I know it's not easy to be in the place of suffering. But I also know from my own life that God will prove Himself faithful if we just surrender ourselves to Him each day in spite of the pain.

I remember thinking so many times that life wasn't worth it. And this was after I knew my destiny and had started doing all I could to achieve it. There were days when it just seemed as if everything and everyone was against me and I had no hope or peace. Everyone around me in my life seemed to have happiness, joy, peace, and hope, but not me. There I was, singing and preaching the Word of God to people who caught hold of it and found the hope they needed, but I didn't have any. It was then that I realized I had to take care of myself, not just offer hope of a better life to those I ministered to. By that, I mean that my own spiritual life wasn't giving me the hope and peace I knew I needed in order to make it in life. So, I started looking after myself and doing those things that strengthened my faith and brought me closer to God each day. Even on days that seemed dark and gloomy and hopeless, I pushed through into the presence of God. He became my Source of peace, joy, faith, and hope. This perseverance in seeking God kept me on the path of destiny, and it gave me hope for the future that I knew was mine by faith.

Destiny

Obviously, it's not an easy thing to live without hope for the future. But we have to believe that God is faithful and that He is able to perform what He has promised (Rom. 4:21). Cheer up, my brothers and sisters who feel that there is no hope for the future, for God is with you, and He loves you with an *"everlasting love"* (Jer. 31:3)! Step out in faith toward your destiny, and do all you can in the now to surrender your lives to Jesus.

Face Up to the Future

Maybe you know there's a destiny for you, and maybe you even have some hope for it. But you're terrified of the future because it seems so big, so daunting. I can understand where you're coming from. Believe me when I tell you that there were days my vision of the future seemed overwhelming and even terrifying. After all, who was I but a young man from the projects? What right did I have to think that I could get out of those projects and become one of the greatest trendsetters in gospel music? I couldn't do it, I thought. It was just too much.

But when those thoughts came, I remembered certain things. I remembered God's faithfulness in the past. I remembered how He miraculously saved me when I was a premature baby given no hope to live. I remembered how He was there to comfort me after my father left. I remembered how He helped my mom get through all those dark days of anger and sadness. I remembered how He gave me a hope and a future in the vision I saw when I was eight years old. I remembered how He strengthened me after my mom's death. I remembered how He set me on this path and gave me the talents to move toward my destiny.

Let me tell you, when you begin to recall all that God has already done in your life and the lives of others, you can't help but buck up and face the future with hope and faith. Look at the God we serve. He's the Creator of the universe. He's the Savior of all mankind. He's the Lord of our lives. He's the Rock we stand on. He's the Father who loves us. He's the Alpha and Omega. He is God Almighty, the Prince of Peace, the King of Kings, the Light of the World, the Good Shepherd, the Bright Morning Star. He's the Way, the Truth, and the Life. God is a good God who wants to bless you as you surrender your life to Him. He will watch over you as you push out into the deep waters of your future. Trust in Him. Believe in Him. Surrender to Him. You will have a peace that passes all understanding (Phil. 4:6–7), and you will be able to look at your future with an excited expectancy.

> When you think of all God has done in your life, you face the future with hope and faith.

Eternity Awaits

Whether we presently have a clear view of our destinies here on earth or not, we can rest in the fact that we all have an eternal destiny in heaven. Knowing that glory awaits us in the life to come can help us keep a focused view of our future in the here and now. You can bet that there will be more times of pain and suffering waiting for you in the future. Actually, Jesus promised we'd face tough times when He said, *"In the world you will have tribulation"* (John 16:33 NKJV). It's not even up for debate. If we are living our lives for Him, we are going to face pain and suffering.

Now, this doesn't exactly sound encouraging when it comes to considering our futures. But that shouldn't matter to us. Jesus also promised us that He would be with us *"to the end of the age"* (Matt. 28:20 NKJV) and that He has overcome the world that causes us pain and suffering (John 16:33). With this in mind, we can confidently know that whenever we come up against tough times in the future, we will not be alone.

Not only that, but we can also look at suffering in life with the attitude that trials bring us into maturity on our destined path. James said to consider it all joy when we come up against trials in life because we know that trials will help us learn patience and will make us *"mature and complete"* (James 1:2–4 NIV). Paul also spoke of the value of trials when he said that tribulations would bring us patience, character, and hope. (See Romans 5:3–4 NRSV). Peter, too, looked at suffering as a way to prove the genuineness of our faith that will result in *"praise, honor, and glory at the revelation of Jesus Christ"* (1 Peter 1:6–7 NKJV).

Peter made an interesting point by talking about *"the revelation of Jesus,"* that great Day when we are all called home. As I just mentioned, we can be confident in our view of the future because our ultimate destiny is to be with Christ in glory. I think Paul said it best when it comes to the suffering we will all face on this earth in relation to the final destiny we will enjoy in heaven. In Romans 8:18, Paul, who suffered beatings, persecution, imprisonment, and many other trials in his life, said, *"I reckon that the sufferings of this present time are not worthy to be compared with the glory which shall be revealed in us."* That's what it's all about! There is absolutely nothing we will face in this life that can be compared to eternal life with Jesus in heaven. There is no trial, no pain, no suffering, no hopelessness, no fear, no sadness, no anguish, nothing that we can compare with the joy of spending the rest of our lives in God's glorious presence!

So, if you are in a place where you just feel as if there is no hope left, remember that God has given you hope for the future. Don't lose your faith in Him, for if you abide in Him, He will strengthen you on your journey to the destined place He has called you to. Remember, what is coming is better than what has been!

Seven

Fatal Attraction

7
Fatal Attraction

For all that is in the world; the lust of the flesh, the lust of the eyes, and the pride of life; is not of the Father but is of the world. And the world is passing away, and the lust of it; but he who does the will of God abides forever.
—1 John 2:16–17 (NKJV)

There is a story about two little boys who went out to fish on the Mississippi River in Arkansas one day. One of the boys, Jimmy, was from a poor farming family who lived in a rural area just a couple of miles from the river. Jimmy didn't have any equipment other than an old fishing pole with a beat-up reel, a bit of line, and a few hooks. The other boy, Reggie, had just moved to the area from the city. He had quickly become friends with Jimmy, who lived up the road from him. Jimmy had been amazed to find out that his new friend had never been fishing before, so he promised to teach Reggie all about fishing. Jimmy had even promised to share his old rod with Reggie so they could both fish a little.

The day finally came that Jimmy and Reggie were able to get away from their chores and go fishing. In the bright sunshine of the late morning, the two boys walked quickly down a local dirt road to a favorite fishing hole of Jimmy's. When they got there, Jimmy hurried to turn over a rotting log, knowing that he would find some choice bait underneath. Sure enough, fat pink worms wriggled in the soft dark soil, and Jimmy scooped up a handful of them and shoved them into his pocket as Reggie stood by and watched.

"Yuck!" Reggie said. "Do I have to touch those things?"

"Only if you want to catch any fish," Jimmy said as he reached into another pocket and dug out a fishing hook.

"I don't like worms," Reggie said.

"I don't either, but the worm ain't gonna put itself on the hook, so somebody has to," Jimmy replied as he tied the hook onto the end of his line.

"Hey, look!" Reggie said.

Jimmy turned around to see Reggie pointing at a shiny gold fishing lure that was hanging down from a branch above them. The lure swung gently back and forth as a warm breeze caught the branch.

"Yeah, that looks like the lure my friend Mike said he got caught in a tree down here when he came down this way last week," Jimmy said as he looked up at the lure, which glistened in the bright sunlight. "He said he didn't feel like cutting it out of there. Mike always was a lazy one!"

Destiny

"Wow! How could you part with such a neat thing like that?" Reggie said as he jumped up to grab at the lure. "Look at how gold and shiny it is. I want to get it!"

"Be careful!" Jimmy shouted.

"Why? I can jump that high, easy!" Reggie said as he jumped up again and put his hand around the lure. "See! I can—Aaaaaaaaaaah!"

Reggie fell to the ground, shaking a bloody right hand.

"I was trying to tell you to watch out for them hooks!" Jimmy said as he wrapped a handkerchief around Reggie's wounded hand and then pointed up at the lure, which was still hanging from the swaying branch. "You can't just go running around in life grabbing at everything that looks good to your eyes, Reggie! Even the prettiest roses got thorns!"

Watch Out!

I think it would be safe to say that the little farm boy in the story was wise beyond his years. I know from experience that it's easy to get caught by things in life that look good but turn out to be deadly. These traps can quickly detour us from our destinies because the enemy will often use such "fatal attractions" to try to draw us away from the plans God has for our lives. This is an area that we need to keep a sharp spiritual eye on so that we can be sensitive to God's leading in even the smallest details of life.

Most of the time, it's pretty easy to see the blatant ways the devil tries to trap us and distract us from destiny. We can point to recreational drugs and say, "Those aren't going to help me reach my destiny." We could do the same for alcohol, violence, sexual sin, murder, and a number of other obvious areas of sin that could lead to our downfall. Satan is crafty, though. He uses these obvious things when he can, but he also uses subtle methods that aren't so easy to detect. Scripture says that he even *"masquerades as an angel of light"* (2 Cor. 11:14 NIV). That means he will disguise his plans to destroy us and make them seem like something that is good for us, something that is attractive. Yet as attractive as the thing may seem to us, it will prove deadly to our destinies.

Satan will use people, objects, situations, and anything else he can to keep us from fulfilling our destinies. He's not God, so he doesn't know our destinies. But he knows that all believers have destinies that will further the kingdom of God, which in turn will weaken his own kingdom of darkness. That's why we have to be on the lookout for things in life that may appear good but will lead only to our destruction.

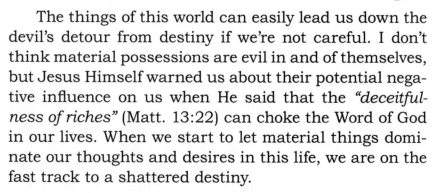

All believers have destinies that will
further the kingdom of God and
weaken the kingdom of darkness.

The things of this world can easily lead us down the devil's detour from destiny if we're not careful. I don't think material possessions are evil in and of themselves, but Jesus Himself warned us about their potential negative influence on us when He said that the *"deceitfulness of riches"* (Matt. 13:22) can choke the Word of God in our lives. When we start to let material things dominate our thoughts and desires in this life, we are on the fast track to a shattered destiny.

Have you heard the story of Achan? He was one of the Israelites who entered the Promised Land in the time of Joshua. He had it good, as all God's people did, in that great land. But it wasn't enough for him. After the tremendous victory at Jericho, Achan took some of the gold, silver, and clothing he found in the city, even though he knew that the Lord had commanded that these items be set aside for His treasury. Joshua, not knowing that Achan had done this, was ready to proceed with conquering the next city. So, he sent the army to Ai, where the Israelites were trounced.

Not understanding why God had allowed the Israelites to taste defeat, Joshua cried out to the Lord in prayer. God told Joshua about the sin in the camp, and Israel's leader quickly did what the Lord commanded to root out the sinner. Achan finally came forward and confessed to what he had done. As the Lord commanded, Achan and all his family were stoned to death and then burned. After that, Joshua and Israel went up and defeated the city of Ai. (See Joshua 7.)

Look at all that Achan's fatal attraction ended up doing to the destinies of those involved. Not only did Achan die, but his wife and children also died because they apparently knew about and condoned his sinful act. Every one of their destinies in God was destroyed by his attraction to the shiny gold and silver he found in Jericho. But that's not all.

Nearly forty Israelites died in the defeat at Ai because of Achan's sin. Every one of their destinies was brought to an end, as well. And what about Israel as a whole? It suffered a major setback in its campaign to conquer the Promised Land. Oh, the Lord made sure that Israel defeated Ai and continued its successful conquest of the land. But it couldn't have been easy for the people to experience a defeat by such a small city as Ai. Even

Joshua began to lose heart after the defeat. (See Joshua 7:6–9.)

That's what the things of this world can do to us and our destinies if we are not careful.

Think how easy it is to get sucked in by people and things that initially seem good but are actually harmful to us. We get to know people who seem to share the same interests and passions in life that we have, and we take them into our lives as friends. We share our destinies with them. We let them see our strengths and our weaknesses. Now, not everyone we know is out to get us. But there are people who come into our lives with only evil in mind. These people may not know they are unwitting tools of the enemy. They may just be out to make a name or fortune for themselves. But at the same time, the enemy will use their relationship with us to bring us down with them. I learned this truth the hard way.

Friendly...Flawless...Fatal

A few years ago, a young man joined our ministry. He wasn't exactly someone who had a lot of natural good looks or anything in the way of the physical that would attract people to him. But he had a certain charm that made everyone like him. Very soon, he had become friends with many people in our ministry. Eventually, I got to know and like him, too. I began to open up to him and invited him to be a part of my destiny. He became acquainted with my friends and family. I explained to him how things were run in the ministry and showed him the resources that I used in my day-to-day activities. There were times when I even provided this man with food, clothing, and shelter that he seemed to need.

After a while, I began to sense that something was going on with this man. There was something about him that just wasn't right. He had become fast friends with my members and colleagues. He had even gotten many of them to believe that he was my right-hand man. I couldn't shake the feeling that something bad had been going on with this man, even though he had become an intricate part of my ministry. I called a week of prayer and fasting at our church. At the end of that week, several people came forward and shared horror stories regarding this man.

It was then that I found out he was manipulating everyone he had befriended in my church. I heard stories of him getting people to pay his rent and buy food and clothing for him as part of his deception. He was able to trick people into letting him use their cars. I also heard stories of seduction. He had coerced many women in the church to have sex with him, leaving some with child, and he had no intentions of supporting the women or children.

I immediately excommunicated this man from our church. Even though I took a lot of heat for it, I knew he had to go. It hit me hard that I had let this man into my destiny. He had manipulated me, my family, my friends, even my gospel music fans. He was a tool of the enemy, and the devil was using him to get me and many others off our destined paths in life.

I never did lose sense of my destiny, and I continued to stay sensitive to the Holy Ghost. He showed me the way out of the manipulative maze created by the enemy. I was able to stay strong in faith as I watched a weapon form against me even though it could not prosper (Isa. 54:17). Still, I should have been more careful to begin with when it came to inviting this man to share in my destiny and be a part of my inner circle of friends. Thankfully, what the devil intended for evil, God turned around for my good. But the end result was still a number of broken people who were hurt by this man. Also, there were many who fell away from God because they persisted in their belief that this man was good. Many couldn't let go of their relationship with him, not knowing that their attraction to him was based on deception and that the end result would prove fatal. All in all, the situation was like hell on earth for me, and this man's effect on my life can still be bitterly felt at times.

Eyes on the Prize

To keep ourselves from falling into the enemy's trap of fatal attractions, we need to remain close to God and abide in His will for our lives. We must turn our backs on the things of this world, even if it means daily denying ourselves things we desire to have. Remember what the apostle John said in his first epistle.

> *Do not love the world or the things in the world. If anyone loves the world, the love of the Father is not in him. For all that is in the world; the lust of the flesh, the lust of the eyes, and the pride of life; is not of the Father but is of the world. And the world is passing away, and the lust of it; but he who does the will of God abides forever.* (1 John 2:15–17 NKJV)

Don't be like Achan, whom we read about earlier. Don't get caught by the fatal attraction that the enemy wants to use to detour you from your destiny. Keep your eyes focused on God, and you will be able to keep yourself from the things of this world that glitter but are not gold. There are always going to be things in this life that are attractive to us in the natural. But just as the little farm boy said, not everything that looks good *is* good for us. We need to use a healthy caution when it comes to being drawn to the things and people that attract us. Remember, we need to crucify our flesh daily (Luke 9:23) so that our desires are the desires that Christ puts in our hearts. In this way, we will be able to understand that fatal attractions are waiting to tempt us and that the enemy wants to use them to detour us from our destinies. But thanks be to God, if we remain in His will at all times, we will continue to press on while walking the path of destiny He has placed us on.

Eight

Betrayal in the Worst Way

8
Betrayal in the Worst Way

They went out from us, but they were not of us; for
if they had been of us, they would no doubt have
continued with us: but they went out, that they might
be made manifest that they were not all of us.
—1 John 2:19

S omeone once told me the story of a woman on the
West Coast who was blindsided by the bitterness
of betrayal. This woman had been married to her
husband for fifteen years, and the two of them had four
children. The family faithfully attended church, and
both mom and dad gave the kids a steady diet of God's
Word at home. The couple's friends all commented on
what a wonderful couple they were and how well they
were raising their children. The woman took it all in,
knowing that she deserved none of the praise because it
had been God's doing to bring her such a godly man for
a husband.

Then, one day, the woman got a phone call in the middle of the day. She picked up the phone and heard her husband's voice through a great deal of static.

"Hello!" she said, wondering why her husband would be calling her when he should be working.

"Yeah, hello!" he answered. "Can you hear me?"

"Yes, dear, but just barely," she said. "It sounds like you're calling from a pay phone."

"I am," he replied.

"Oh, did you go out for your lunch break today?"

"No, I didn't go to work today."

"What do you mean?" she asked. "Where are you?"

"I'm in Texas."

"What! What are you doing there?"

"I'm on my way to Atlanta. I wanted to call to let you know."

"Atlanta! Why? What's going on, honey? Why do you have to go to Atlanta?"

"Uh, well, I'm meeting someone there."

"Who?! Who's there that you know?"

The woman waited as the static crackled in her ear.

"I met a woman on the Internet six months ago," he said. "I'm driving out to be with her. I'll be sending you the divorce papers to sign once I've moved in with her."

The woman dropped the phone and started crying.

"Are you still there?" she heard her husband yell from the phone, which lay on the counter next to her.

She picked up the phone with a shaking hand.

"How...how could you?" she cried. "You said...you said you loved me. How dare you do this to me and the children! My God, how could you do this to us! How? How could you do it?"

The woman slammed the phone down and slumped to the floor, where she began screaming.

"Oh, God! How could he do it? How could he?" she cried out as the tears rolled down her face. "How could he betray us? How, God?"

Bitterness of Betrayal

I don't know what your life has been like, but I hope you have never had to go through something like this woman did. Can you imagine the wrenching pain that must have shot through her heart when her husband told her of his betrayal? This woman had her life torn apart in a matter of seconds. When she picked up the phone, she probably had all she wanted in life. She had most likely given her husband a kiss good-bye that morning and then watched him drive off to work. But when she slammed the phone down after talking with him that afternoon, her world had been turned upside down. The person she had called her husband was now the man who had betrayed her. She had been forced to swallow the bitter pill of betrayal, and it had left her crying on the floor in pain and anguish.

This story reminds me of the sad events that were set into motion during the last days Jesus was on this earth before He was crucified. Doesn't it break your heart when you read the story of Judas giving Jesus a kiss in the Garden of Gethsemane? (See Luke 22:47–48.) Can you imagine the pain and sadness that Jesus must have felt at that moment? Think about it.

Jesus had brought Judas into His inner circle of disciples. He had lovingly taught him the Word of God. He had performed astonishing miracles in front of him. He had given him charge of the money box. Jesus may even have allowed Judas to hear His most intimate conversations with the Father in times of prayer.

But what happened when the Jewish officials were trying to find a way to seize Jesus and put Him to death?

Judas betrayed the One who loved him.

I fully understand that Jesus knew about Judas' betrayal before it happened. (See John 6:70–71; 13:21–27.) But I don't think that knowledge made getting stabbed in the back by one of His disciples any easier. Judas still had a free will, and he could have chosen not to betray the Lord. But he did.

We may also face the bitterness of betrayal. There are probably going to be people who come into our lives whom we think are a part of our destiny. We may find out the hard way that they were simply tools of the enemy in his attempt to detour us from our destiny. They will turn on us. They will betray us. They will hurt us. The pain of betrayal stings, and it has the potential to leave in us a bitterness toward people and life.

But if we are going to stay on the path of destiny, we will have to move past the bitterness and pain of betrayal. Not only will we have to forget about the people who betrayed us, but we will also have to forgive them and release them into the hands of God. I know all too well how much betrayal hurts.

I remember when I had to deal with a spirit of betrayal that came from those closest to me. It was a most horrifying experience. Because I was undergoing attacks from people outside my camp, I never thought to look inside the camp to discover the trouble. I was so convinced that there was an outside force working against me and the church that I decided to quit singing and preaching in the New York area. I also cut off fellowship with some churches in the area in an attempt to flush out the cancer that I felt was growing on our ministry by this outside force, not knowing that the real problem was internal, not external.

But even after I had taken such drastic measures, the bad feeling in my spirit never left. So, I began to walk on pins and needles in my interactions with everyone around me, even with those family members and friends closest to me. Every day, it seemed as if there was something new trying to assault me, trying to destroy everything God had given me. From my church to my family, from my sanity to my health, it seemed as if the devil was pouring pain on me. I isolated myself from everyone, went before God, and sought His wisdom. The Scriptures came alive to me, and I could relate to what Jesus must have felt as Judas betrayed Him. Even though I didn't know who the betrayer in my life was, I began to sense that it was someone close to me. Yet after the week of prayer and fasting that uncovered the man we discussed in the previous chapter as the instigator of it all, it still wasn't over.

I began to find out many of those closest to me had been sucked into this man's evil scheme to destroy me. Even worse, I discovered that the gossip and lies about me that had spread throughout the city had come from them—words that were meant to smear my name and bring me down. I encountered jealousy and envy from people I never would have thought twice about trusting my life with. I couldn't believe it. I was angry. I was bitter. I felt a desperate loneliness.

The loneliness only got worse as I did what I knew I had to do to rectify the entire situation. I bid farewell to those closest to me, and I released them from my own life into the hands of God. I accepted the fact that these people had been deceived into becoming part of the enemy's plan to detour me from my destiny. I had to digest the truth of that before I could go on with my life. It left me with a loneliness and an emptiness that I can't describe, but God was faithful. He sent me people who came alongside me and ministered to me. They helped me stay focused on what God had called me to do, and they proved themselves to be true family and friends when it came to supporting me on my path of destiny.

It Can Happen to Anyone

Betrayal can happen to anyone. Sure, we can all feel betrayed by elected officials when they do something contrary to what they had promised us. That kind of betrayal can leave us a little confused and angry, but it rarely stings us with a bitter pain. The sort of betrayal I'm talking about comes from those who are close to us. It comes from those who are supposed to support us and love us no matter what. It comes from people we think are a part of our destiny.

Betrayal in the worst way comes from those closest to us. Only those we love and believe inflict upon us the bitterest betrayal. They are the ones who are supposed to support us no matter what the cost. They are supposed to help us in the areas of our lives in which we could use some help. They are supposed to be there for us when the chips are down. They are supposed to protect us from the attacks of the enemy. They are supposed to stand up for our names and our character when we are falsely accused.

In my case, many of those closest to me did just the opposite. They tried to bring me down. They furthered the enemy's plan to destroy me. They besmirched my name when they had the opportunity. They attempted to make public some faults of mine that should have remained private. What's worse, many of those who betrayed me were people whom I had *invited* to be a part of my destiny. I had invited them into my life to be a part of what God had called me to do. I had brought them into my so-called inner circle. I had shared with them—my hopes, my dreams, my flaws, everything there was to know about me. Then, when the enemy used this man in the church to get to me, these people, who were supposed to be closest to me, turned on me and betrayed me.

I understand what the apostle John was saying in his first epistle when he wrote, *"They went out from us, but they were not of us; for if they had been of us, they would no doubt have continued with us: but they went out, that they might be made manifest that they were not all of us"* (1 John 2:19). He was talking about people who leave our lives and betray us, proving that they were really never a part of us in the sense of our destinies. They may have seemed to us at the time as if they were, but when it came right down to it, they turned their backs on us when we needed them the most. That's the kind of betrayal that hurts in the worst way. I believe that we will all probably face betrayal from such people. It's sad, too, because in my case, the people who were trying to wreck my destiny may very well have ruined their own destinies in the process.

Part of the Plan?

I believe that some of the people I have been talking about were most definitely supposed to be a part of my destiny. Of course, they had their own destinies, as well. I think God would have seen to it that our destinies would have intersected in such a way as to move all of us closer to what God had planned for our lives. It goes

> All our individual destinies fit together into God's perfect plan for His body.

back to what I said about corporate destiny. All of our individual destinies fit together into God's perfect plan for His body, the church. As long as we stay focused on Him and His will for our individual lives, He will make sure that our destinies merge into something that furthers His kingdom here on earth.

But when we lose sight of our destinies, or when we fall into a trap of the enemy, we start to hinder not only our own destinies but also the destinies of those around us. In my situation, God gave me grace to keep surrendering my life to Him, in spite of the fact that many of those around me were starting to fall off the paths of their own destinies while trying to destroy mine. I was fortunate to stay on the path of my destiny, even with all the enemy was doing in the lives of those closest to me.

Remember the story of Achan from the last chapter? When he stole gold, silver, and clothing from the vanquished city of Jericho, he was doing more than just disobeying the Lord's commandment regarding sacred articles. He was also betraying the people of Israel. Think about what the families in the tents next to his thought after they learned Achan had sinned in a way that brought God's judgment on Israel in the form of defeat at Ai. They were probably furious that Achan had done such a wicked thing. Achan had also had a destiny in God; he had been a part of the Lord's plan for Israel's conquest of the Promised Land. His individual destiny could have been an integral part of Israel's becoming its own nation. But he lost his focus and betrayed his brethren. Thankfully, Joshua sought the Lord's guidance in this situation, and Achan's sin did not derail the Israelites' destiny to inhabit the Promised Land.

 How do we get over the bitter pain of betrayal? Forgiveness.

The Way Out

Physically separating ourselves from those who have betrayed us may not be all that hard. In many cases, it's simply a matter of walking away from them. What may not be so easy is dealing with the pain these people leave us in the wake of their betrayal. I know the pain is real. It hurts. It's bitter. It stings to think about people we once considered close after they have betrayed us. But the pain of betrayal has to be dealt with if we are to seize our destinies and go after them with our whole hearts. The bitterness of betrayal only hinders us in our walks with God and on our journeys toward destiny.

So, what's the answer? How do we get over the bitter pain of betrayal? The answer is not simple, nor is it easy.

Yet it all comes down to one word: forgiveness. If we can forgive, God can heal even the bitterest pain in our lives. Forgiving is probably one of the hardest things we will ever do in this life. Still, it's a command of Jesus. He told us in one of His many parables that if we do not forgive those who sin against us, we will be dealt with severely by God the Father. (See Matthew 18:20–35.) He also taught us in the Lord's Prayer to forgive others, and afterward went on to say that the Father will not forgive our sins if we don't forgive the sins of others (Matt. 6:12, 14–15). That's some serious talk on forgiveness. I believe Jesus said what He meant when He commanded us to forgive each other.

There is an amazing power in forgiveness. Going back to the parable Jesus told about forgiveness, we see that one servant was forgiven an enormous debt owed to the king. But when that same servant went out and found another servant who owed him a small amount of money, he violently demanded that the man should pay him back. When the man said he couldn't, the servant who had been forgiven his own enormous debt to the king had the man thrown into debtor's prison. When the king found out about it, he was furious, and he cast into debtor's prison the servant he had just forgiven of his debt. (See Matthew 18:20–35.)

Here's a good question that not too many people probably think of when reading this passage: At the conclusion of the parable, who ends up in prison? The answer is *both* servants mentioned in the story. The servant who had been forgiven so much by the king and the man he himself wouldn't forgive are both in jail. That's the kind of bondage that unforgiveness can bring into our lives and the lives of those whom we won't forgive.

Destiny

Unforgiveness shackles us in our own spiritual walk and keeps us from fulfilling the destiny for our lives. This is so sad, but true.

Betrayal is a hard thing for us to face. The answer to going on after being betrayed is not much easier. Forgiveness takes the grace of God, and it takes some serious work on our parts to move past the pain and do what God commanded us to do. If we are going to keep our destinies squarely in our sights, we must practice the command of Jesus and forgive those who have sinned against us.

Betrayal hurts; there is no doubt about it. It's painful. It's bitter. It's something I hope I never have to go through again in my life. But the chances are that we will all face some sort of betrayal in our lives. Whatever the degree of betrayal, we will feel its pain. I want to challenge you not to let the pain stop you on your path to destiny. You need to learn forgiveness and then just release the person or people who betrayed you into the hands of God. Don't let someone's evil action ruin your journey to destiny. Rise above it, and draw near to God. He will give you the grace and strength to go on and achieve all that He has planned for you.

Nine

Fear Factor

9
Fear Factor

For God hath not given us the spirit of fear; but of
power, and of love, and of a sound mind.
—2 Timothy 1:7

My journey into ministering the Word of God as a pastor was one that I did not want to take in the natural. I had been singing for years, ministering in that realm and feeling very comfortable in it. I could stand in front of thousands of people and sing the praises of the Lord with no problem. But when the call of God came to begin preaching His Word, as well as pastoring, I shuddered in fear at the thought of it.

Pastoring a church was an entirely different area of ministry, and I just couldn't get over the paralyzing anxiety that anticipating this change was bringing to my life. All I could think of was the responsibility I would bear for all those souls in my care as a shepherd of God's flock. I might someday be pastoring hundreds and hundreds of people, maybe even thousands. I didn't want that kind of pressure. It was too much for me to handle.

As if that wasn't enough, I also struggled with the fear of having to know God's Word inside out. As a singer, I had delved into God's Word and studied it for my own growth. But as a pastor, I would not only have to study the Word but also know it thoroughly enough to teach it to men, women, and children searching for the answers to life. Again, I didn't want that kind of pressure.

And that still wasn't all. The Love Fellowship Choir and I were growing in our popularity within the body of Christ as well as outside the church. We were accepted by our fans with love and open arms. It was a good feeling knowing that there were always going to be people cheering us on. But when it came to the thought of being a pastor, fear took its toll—I was untried, and I would be alone on the stage. All I could think about was the possible rejection I would face from the people in the church. What if they didn't like what I had to say? And how would I come up with a sermon to preach every week?

You can probably tell that I wasn't exactly diving right in as far as taking up the call of God in my life to be a pastor. I had fears that crippled me, keeping me from moving forward in my calling. I was in my comfort zone when I was singing. I was being effective in an area to which God had called me. But I knew that my previous success didn't make running from this new call right in God's sight. In fact, I knew I couldn't run from it. Jonah ran from the call of God, and he ended up being swallowed by a whale before he did what he was supposed to do. I knew that no one ever really ran from God without facing up to Him at some point down the line. So, I finally did what I knew I had to do.

Destiny

I stepped out in faith.

I was praying one day, and I felt the words of Philippians 4:13 rise up in my spirit: *"I can do all things through Christ which strengtheneth me."* Right then and there, I stood up and surrendered to God's call to be a preacher. I knew it was part of my destiny. I knew it was the next stage of the journey in God's plan for my life. And I knew I would live in sorrow and regret if I tried to deny what God was calling me to do. So, I dove into my destiny headfirst, knowing that God would care for me as He always had. And He did.

God was patient with me as I learned His Word in a new way. He gave me grace in learning to speak in front of others. In addition, He must have given my flock grace in those first days that I stood up and spoke to them as a young pastor trying to teach from the Scriptures. But He also gave me a strong support network of family and friends who were there with me every step of the way, encouraging and sustaining me in every way they could. God was faithful. I grew as a pastor, and our flock began to increase by leaps and bounds as people came into our church and heard the salvation message being preached. Now, we have two churches, one in Brooklyn and one in Bensalem, Pennsylvania; and we are starting another in Newark, New Jersey. I know this is not my doing. It's all God's doing. Still, if I had allowed my fears about being a pastor to control me, I could have slowed down this great work of God, and many of those who have been saved through our ministry might be lost today because of my fear.

It's Frightening

Fear is a real feeling. It can actually sometimes be a beneficial feeling. If you have ever been chased by a ferocious dog, you know what I'm talking about. That sort of fear is the healthy reaction to a situation that warrants caution—and quick action. It is almost like an internal radar system that warns us of possible danger in our lives. But that's obviously not the kind of fear I'm talking about now.

No, the kind of fear I'm referring to is the kind that paralyzes you in your life's journey and halts you on your way to destiny. It rears its ugly head, shakes a finger in your face, and then says something like, "You can't do it because you're not smart enough," or "Who do you think you are, believing you could do such a great thing?" This kind of fear comes straight out of the kingdom of darkness, and the devil wields it as a mighty sword against the saints.

I've often heard it said that stress is the number one killer in our lives. I'm sure stress is something many people have to battle against, but I would venture to say that fear is even more deadly than stress. In the physical realm, fear can paralyze our minds and break down our bodies with the weight of anxiety in our lives. In the spiritual realm, it is even more dangerous. In that area, fear can keep us in complete bondage, unable to draw near to God and walk in His will for our lives. When fear grips our minds and hearts, it's as if we have spiritual shackles on because we blind ourselves to God's love and power when we live in fear.

But fear is something that we will all face in our lives because there are always opportunities to grow afraid. We can fear the future and all it holds. Or we can fear the future because we think it holds nothing for us. We can fear not making enough money or being laid off from our jobs. We can fear not being adequate as parents or as children or as friends or as employees. We can fear those around us, always living on pins and needles because we think that someone is out to get us or our jobs or what we own. I struggled in this area for years. Or, we can fear change in our lives. We can fear stagnation. We can fear doing new things. We can fear failure. We can even fear accomplishing too much because of the responsibility it will bring us. The list can go on and on, and I have dealt with many of these fear factors in my own life.

Fear's effect on our lives is always the same. Again, it stops us dead in our tracks on the journey to our destinies. Fear is a weapon the devil has used against God's people since the days of old. Let's look at what fear did to the Israelites who came out of Egypt.

As we saw earlier when looking at Joshua's life, the Israelites had come out of Egypt and were preparing to enter the Promised Land. Moses sent twelve spies to search out the land before waging war against it. The spies returned and reported that the land was an amazing place filled with the "milk and honey" that God had promised them. They also brought back some of the land's choicest fruit and showed it to all the Israelites, who must have marveled at the richness of the land.

But the spies also brought back news of the people who lived there. They told the Israelites of mighty warriors and giants who made them look like grasshoppers. Except for Joshua and Caleb, all the spies went on and on about how the inhabitants of the Promised Land would just crush the Israelites and devour them. Joshua and Caleb, on the other hand, said that it didn't matter who lived in the land because God was well able to deliver all their enemies into their hands. Now, at this point, the Israelites had a choice to make. They could go along with what Joshua and Caleb said and surrender themselves to God and His destiny for their lives, or they could believe the negative report the other spies brought back and live in fear.

They chose fear, and God was not happy with them at all. The children of Israel sat in their tents that night, crying and whining about how terrible it would be to go forward and get wiped out by the "giants" the spies had seen. They even went so far as to say that life would be better back in Egypt, where they had lived as slaves under the oppressive rule of Pharaoh. Fear of what they might face paralyzed them. It stopped them from moving forward, conquering the Promised Land, and taking hold of the destiny that God had planned for them. It turned almost all of them into whimpering cowards who missed out on God's blessing in a major way because the Lord judged them for their lack of faith in His proven ability to deliver them. Since the Israelites' fear was greater than their faith, all the Israelites over twenty years old, except for Joshua and Caleb, were condemned to die in the desert over the next forty years. It took that long before all the people whose fear prevented the nation of Israel from entering into God's destiny for them were dead. (See Numbers 13–14.)

That's what fear can do to us. It can stop us from fulfilling our destinies, if we let it. It can send us to our deaths spiritually, if we let it. It's a sad thing, but it happens all too often.

On Thin Ice?

I heard a story of a father and son who were driving down to the river one cold winter day. Bouncing along in their old pickup truck, they drove down an old dirt road that led them right to the riverbank, where they stopped and got out.

Looking out over the icy white river, the little boy shook his head and then turned to his father and said, "I thought you said we were going to cross the river at the end of this dirt road. I don't see no bridge, though, Dad."

The father smiled as he gazed out across the river. Then, he looked back at his son and said, "We don't need a bridge, son. We're going to drive across the river itself."

"What!" the little boy exclaimed. "But we'll crash through the ice in the truck and drown, Dad!"

The father chuckled, then put a hand on his son's shoulder. "No, son. You know I wouldn't do anything that would put you in that kind of danger."

"Yeah, I know," the boy said. "But I'm afraid the ice is going to break!"

"Well, I can understand that. But listen here," the father said. "The ice on this river is so thick right now that we could probably drive a dump truck over it and not worry about falling in."

The little boy looked back out across the ice as if to study it to see if what his father said could be true. Then, the little boy looked back up at his father and said, "Wow! It's really that thick! Neat, Dad. Let's get going!"

The father and son climbed back into the truck and started out across the ice. The father drove slowly, and the little boy let out "oohs" and "ahs" as they traversed the icy sheet. About halfway across the river, the little boy pointed upriver and said, "Look, Dad!"

The father peered up the icy river and saw a man on his hands and knees crawling across the river slowly, stopping every few feet to look back at the shore.

"What is he doing, Dad?" the little boy asked.

"I suppose he's just trying to get across the river, like we are," the father replied. "Looks scared, doesn't he?"

"Yeah, he sure does," the little boy said as he continued to stare out his window at the man. "But why is he so afraid, Dad?"

"Well, he doesn't trust the ice, like you didn't at first when I told you about driving across the river," the father answered. "So, he's afraid of what might happen to him even though it never will."

"That's too bad," the little boy said as his father pulled the pickup truck onto the opposite shore from where they had started. "It must be sad to live like that, huh, Dad?"

"I couldn't have said it better myself, son," the father replied.

False Evidence Appearing Real

The little boy was correct in his assessment of the man who crawled across the river in fear. It's sad to hear of someone letting fear cripple him in life. But that's how it is with so many of us. We rely on what we see and let fear rule our lives instead of walking by faith and not by sight (2 Cor. 5:7). Living in fear is an easy thing to do because fear looks only at the circumstances. Faith demands that we trust God instead of what we see around us. Our natural tendency is to lean on the flesh rather than on what God has said or done in the past. The saddest thing about this inclination is the fact that most of the fears we have are completely unfounded.

I like to think of fear as an acronym. F-E-A-R: False Evidence Appearing Real. That's just what fear is to believers. We have God's Word. We know that He promises to protect us. We know that He promises to provide for us. We know that He loves and cares for us. Yet, too often, instead of believing these things by faith, we believe in the evidence of our circumstances, and we let fear rule our lives. Our fears are founded on nothing but the things we imagine could happen and the things that are contrary to God's Word and promises. They're false. They're not real. They just *appear* real to our minds, and so we run with them. We lean on our own understanding instead of trusting the Lord with our whole hearts (Prov. 3:5).

I remember visiting South Africa a few years ago to do a concert. One day, when we had some free time, we took a bus tour of the local region. We were amazed to see just how far black people had come since apartheid ended. People who were once oppressed and downtrodden were now living in comfortable homes and driving nice cars. They had taken advantage of the opportunity presented to them after so many years of living in persecution and near-poverty.

However, as we drove a short distance outside town, we came to a small village. I was astonished to see young children running around, filthy, while their parents sat in front of the small huts they called home. We stopped in the village and talked with the kids and their parents. I couldn't believe what I was seeing and hearing. These people had no indoor plumbing, no clean running water of any sort, no electricity. They were living in dirty shacks. It was unbelievable to me that such a place could exist just a stone's throw from the beautiful homes we had just seen.

After saying good-bye to the villagers, we all boarded the bus again. I started to become angry that these people had to live in such abject poverty, so I asked the tour guide how such a place could still exist now that the oppression in the nation had ended.

He replied, "All those people could be just as well-off as the other people we've seen. They live in poverty like that because they want to."

I shook my head in disbelief. "Why?"

"Because they are afraid to try something they don't know," he replied. "They would rather live in the comfort of their poverty than step out and do something that could bring them into prosperity."

I couldn't believe it! But then, I remembered my own experience when it came to heeding God's call to preach. My hesitance to be a pastor was similar to the man crawling across the river of ice and the people in the South African village. I hadn't wanted to do what God had called me to do because I was afraid of something I imagined to be terrifying. As I sat on that bus, I began to understand that fear could paralyze anyone in any situation.

Fight the Fear

My brothers and sisters, fear is a killer of destiny. Destiny demands that we keep walking the path God has called us to, even when we can't see what is waiting just around the corner. Destiny demands that we take leaps of faith throughout our lives. And that is where the answer to fighting fear is found—in faith.

Destiny

The Bible clearly states that God did not give us a spirit of fear, but rather one of power, love, and a sound mind (2 Tim. 1:7). When we are in God, we have His love, and we have a sound mind. We can think clearly in the midst of fear and understand that, because He loves us, we can step out in His power and take a step of faith *over* fear. Is this easy? No. But we can do it. We have to do it if we are to achieve our destinies in God.

We must meditate on the Bible verses that speak of God's power in our lives, and we must remember the people in Scripture who took a step of faith and believed God, even when the circumstances they faced could have paralyzed them with fear.

Think about David when he faced Goliath. Goliath was a giant of a man who stood about nine feet tall. Day after day, he had come to challenge the Israelites to battle. And day after day, the Israelites had cowered in fear of the giant who stood before them. Then, along came David—just a young shepherd boy. He saw Goliath and asked why no one had gone out to fight him. When he heard that no one had the courage to face the Philistine champion, he became angered that such a heathen could keep the people of God cowering in fear. He quickly went out to meet Goliath in battle, taking only a sling and some stones as his weapons.

Goliath, of course, laughed at David, then cursed him by his gods and promised to feed David's body to the birds. David, irate that the Philistine would dare challenge and mock the God of Israel, shouted back to Goliath that God was on the side of Israel and that it would be the giant who would be fed to the birds by the hand of the Lord. The two rushed to meet in battle, and David hurled a stone with his sling.

The stone sank into Goliath's forehead, killing him, and David led Israel to a great victory that day. What thousands of mighty warriors couldn't do because of the fear that gripped them, a young shepherd boy did with a child's weapon and a heart that trusted in God.

David didn't let the fear that paralyzed everyone else get to him. He chose to believe in the power of God instead. He remembered that, in past days, God had delivered him from the lion and the bear while he was tending sheep. David figured that, if God had done it before, He would do it again. So, he stepped out in faith and chose to rely on His God to decide the outcome, and God came through for David. (See 1 Samuel 17.)

That's the kind of faith I'm talking about! We need the kind of faith David had. But how do we get it? By doing basic things that will help us grow in the Lord. We need to pray and get close to God so that we can know Him so intimately that we will never doubt His love or power in our lives. We need to read the Bible so that we can internalize His Word and have it ready whenever fear rears its ugly heads in our lives. We need to fellowship with other believers so that we can be a vital part of the army of God. By doing these things consistently and faithfully, we can overcome fear whenever we face it in life.

A quick word study in the King James Version of the Bible reveals two interesting phrases that are used over and over when it comes to people dealing with being afraid. The words *"fear not"* and *"be not afraid"* occur ninety-one times in the Bible. In most of these instances, the Lord is speaking these words to someone who is ready to give in to fear. There was Abraham, whom God encouraged with the words "Fear not" when the father of our faith was still childless and without an heir (Gen. 15:1). There was Joshua, who heard God speak the words *"Be not afraid"* when he was preparing to lead the Israelites into the Promised Land (Josh. 1:9). There was Isaiah, through whom the Lord said *"Fear not"* to the downtrodden Israelites (Isa. 41:13). There was the Virgin Mary, who heard God say through an angel *"Fear not"* when she discovered she was with child (Luke 1:30). There was the apostle Paul, who heard the words *"Be not afraid"* from the Lord when he was being persecuted for preaching the Gospel (Acts 18:9). And finally, there was the apostle John, who, as an exile on the isle of Patmos, heard Jesus say *"Fear not"* when the Lord appeared to him in all His glorious might (Rev. 1:17).

The Lord is whispering such words in our own spirits when we are afraid. As we can see by those examples, fear can grip people through a number of circumstances. But in each case, God says, in essence, the same thing: "Fear not, my child. I am with you. Be not afraid, because I will be your peace and your strength." Oh, it's often hard to hear these sweet words when fear is screaming in our spirits. That's why we need to get our eyes off what is causing our fears and put them back on God and His promises to us. And that's why we really need to understand how to walk by faith and not by sight.

So, when you are living in fear of something or someone, remember the words of our Lord: "Fear not," and "Be not afraid." Then consider the old saying, "Fear knocked at the door. Faith answered. No one was there!" That's what faith in God will do to the fear in your life as you journey on to destiny each day.

Ten

Family and Friends

10
Family and Friends

Two are better than one; because they have a good reward for their labour. For if they fall, the one will lift up his fellow: but woe to him that is alone when he falleth; for he hath not another to help him up.
—Ecclesiastes 4:9–10

I have to admit that when I began to get seriously involved with the church as a teen, my family and friends didn't exactly jump right on board to support me. I kept on going to church because I just knew that whatever I would accomplish in life would come through the church. But my family and friends poked fun at me for wanting to get involved with church. After all, church wasn't exactly the happening place for a teen to be. They all figured it was merely some phase I was going through.

Yet, as I said, I knew my destiny would come only through the church. So, even though I didn't have my family or friends backing me, I pressed on toward what

I knew was my destiny. I went after it by going to church every week and learning all I could and singing every chance I got. I kept getting closer to God and, along the way, I began to better understand His will for me. When my family and friends saw that going to church wasn't just a phase in my life, they quit teasing me about it and started giving me their complete support. I remember my sister Viola saying to me, "Hezekiah, I'm proud of you. You can do it!"

Amazing! What a difference their support made in my life. I was ready to forsake everyone to follow the call of God. That meant my family, my friends, and everyone else. But when those closest to me gave me their love and support in this endeavor, it was like a gust of fresh wind to help carry me along on my destined journey.

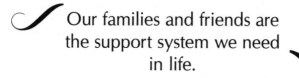 Our families and friends are the support system we need in life.

That's the kind of support system we all need in order to fulfill God's plan for our lives. Our families and friends can make all the difference when it comes to making it through those times when life just doesn't seem fair and when the days are darkest.

Friends Forever

You usually know those whom you can truly count on when you need them most. Every single one of our friends should be important to us. When you are at your lowest point in life and think you just can't go on, that's when your closest and most faithful friends will be there to lift you up again. It's these kinds of friends who will help you stay strong on your journey to destiny.

I don't think there is a better story of friendship in the Bible than that of Jonathan and David. It's a story that shows what a true friend is, and it also proves how important such a friend can be to an individual achieving his or her destiny.

In the days when Saul was king of Israel, David was just a shepherd boy looking after his father's few sheep in the wilderness. Because Saul had grieved the Lord's heart with his sins, God decided to anoint a new king of Israel. That new king was to be David. The prophet Samuel came to David and anointed him as the next king of Israel, even though he would not become king for many years. After David killed Goliath, Saul took David into his own house. David and Saul's son Jonathan became fast friends. They even entered into a covenant of friendship.

Eventually, Saul began to take offense at David, for he knew that David was a threat to his throne. Saul went so far as to try to kill David in the palace, but David escaped and fled from him. Jonathan found David and encouraged him, telling him that he would smooth things over with his father. And he did. Soon, David was back in the palace serving the king. But again, Saul became angry with David. He was jealous of the success David was having in life, so, once more, he tried to kill him.

When David fled into the wilderness to hide from Saul, Jonathan searched for him and found him. The two talked about David's precarious situation, and Jonathan again swore his undying friendship to David. He then went back to the palace to learn just how intent his father was on killing David. When Jonathan confronted Saul about it, the king became enraged. He screamed at

Jonathan, saying, "Don't you know that if David lives, you'll never become king!" Then, Saul tried to kill his own son by hurling a spear at him.

Jonathan went back to David and told him that the king did indeed intend to kill him. They both wept greatly, for they knew the time had come for them to part ways. After they reminded each other about their covenant of friendship, Jonathan bid David farewell, perhaps realizing he would never see his friend again. Eventually, Saul and Jonathan were killed in battle against the Philistines, and David did become king of the land. Upon learning that Jonathan had died, David cried and said, *"I grieve for you, Jonathan my brother; you were very dear to me. Your love for me was wonderful, more wonderful than that of women"* (2 Sam. 1:26 NIV). (See 1 Samuel 16:1–13; 18–20.)

That's the kind of friendship I'm talking about! In David's case, his bond with Jonathan exceeded even his spousal relationships. He considered his friend to be as close as a brother. And look at how much Jonathan thought of David. Even though he was the son of the king and heir to the throne, he still supported his friend on his destined path toward becoming the next king. These kinds of friends are very rare, but when they come into our lives, we must be thankful for their presence and for their being a blessing to us on our journeys to destiny. We must appreciate their ministry to us and allow them to strengthen us when we are feeling weak.

We need to be open and honest in our friendships. We must be transparent so that we can understand our friends and they can understand us. This can be a risky thing, because, as we saw in an earlier chapter, some friends turn out to be enemies used by the devil. Still, we need to trust God when it comes to growing close to those around us. We will be blessed by faithful friends, and we should also be a blessing to them in their own journeys toward destiny. Friends are a wonderful gift from God, and their influence should not be underestimated in regard to helping us go after and achieve our destinies.

If you feel as if you just don't have any friends in life, they are only a prayer away. God can send you the perfect friends so that you will enjoy the wonderful love that comes with a close friendship. You will be a blessing to them, and they will be a blessing to you, as well.

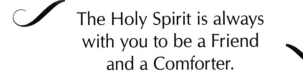

> The Holy Spirit is always
> with you to be a Friend
> and a Comforter.

And never forget that the Holy Spirit is always with you to be a Friend and a Comforter. He is the perfect Friend, always ready to support and encourage you but never afraid to gently warn or convict you when you're heading down the wrong path. So often, we forget about the work of the Holy Spirit in our lives. But He is real, He is God, and He lives in us. Don't forget about Him; talk to Him every day and learn to know His voice and enjoy the wonderful friendship that He offers you.

Family Matters

Family is also a vital help for moving us toward destiny. For those of you who have families who support and love you in all you do, you know it is an incredible feeling to have such a support system. When the chips are down, you know you can rely on your family. You can go to them for advice and guidance. You know they will listen to you with loving hearts. If they are believers, you can ask them to pray for you, and you know they will seek God's face on your behalf. That kind of support system can do wonders in helping you achieve your destiny in life.

Now, I understand that not everyone is going to have such a supportive family. Some of you live with family members who are indifferent to you. They don't criticize you, but they don't exactly support you, either. Others of you have families who do nothing but tear you down. They criticize you every chance they get, and they laugh at your dreams and goals in life. Still others of you don't have families at all, for one reason or another, and you long to belong to a family who will love and support you.

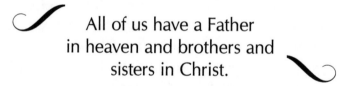

All of us have a Father
in heaven and brothers and
sisters in Christ.

Whatever your situation might be, I want you to know that God understands your hurt and your desire to have a family that will be there for you. He will provide the family you need. He will give you friends who will become like family to you, and who will become an integral part of your journey toward destiny. God is faithful, dear brothers and sisters, and He will see to it that you have the support system you need when it comes to family.

All of us must also remember that we belong to the family of God and that our brothers and sisters in Christ will be there for us to enable us to fulfill our destinies. In addition, we have a Father in heaven who loves us and is always with us. Let us never forget that, in the journey of life, the family of God and the Father Himself will support us in our darkest times. Let us also remember that we have a Friend who sticks closer than a brother (Prov. 18:24). The Lord Jesus Himself promised to be with us to the end of the age (Matt. 28:20). He is someone we can count on to be there to lift us up when the going gets rough in life. Knowing that He's on our side makes all the difficult times easier to bear. With this assurance, we can confidently step out in faith and journey toward destiny, no matter what our situations in life.

"Do to Others"

Ultimately, when it comes to family and friends, we need to remember the Golden Rule found in Matthew 7:12. In this verse, Jesus told us, *"Do to others what you would have them do to you"* (NIV). If we expect just to receive love and support without ever offering it ourselves, we'll soon find that we have become self-centered, always wanting but never giving.

If we allow that to happen to us, we will become like the pond that a little girl was puzzled over. This little girl had been going to a nearby pond to fish and play for years. But one day when she came to the pond, she noticed a dead fish floating on the water. The next day, she saw another dead fish. Then, a few days later, she noticed that a thin layer of green film was starting to form at the edges of the pond. Finally, she asked her father to come out and see if he could fix the pond.

When the father arrived, he took one glance at the pond and immediately began to walk to the other end of it. The little girl quickly followed along, eager to see what her dad was going to do. The father finally stopped and stooped down at the edge of the pond. He reached out and pushed on a large log that was lying across the mouth of a small creek that had been flowing out of the pond. After a few minutes of pushing, the father had moved the log completely out of the mouth of the creek. Immediately, water from the pond began to flow down the dry creek bed.

"What happened, Dad?" the little girl asked.

"I suppose that old log must have somehow rolled down that hill and become caught right here at the head of the creek," the father replied. "That's what was making the pond go bad."

"How come?" the little girl asked.

"Well, the pond was getting fresh water from the little stream on the other end, but it didn't have anywhere to let water flow out because of the log."

"So?" the little girl said.

"Honey, if a pond doesn't have an outlet, it becomes what is called 'stagnant.' And then the pond begins to go bad, and it can't support life anymore."

This story illustrates exactly what I'm talking about in regard to allowing God's love, grace, and provision to flow into us and then out of us as a blessing to others. We will become stagnant like the pond if we aren't blessing others with what God has given us. We will become incapable of enjoying the life of Christ within us because we will lose sight of God Himself and think only of His blessings in our lives.

It's a sad thing to see the people of God feeding themselves but never feeding others. I have to tell you that, if you just take in life, the day will come when there will be nothing left to take from. We must remember the words of Proverbs 11:25: *"The generous soul will be made rich, and he who waters will also be watered himself"* (NKJV). There seems to be a spiritual dynamic that demands that we be givers if we ourselves want to be blessed in life. If we are generous, God will bless us. If we water the souls of others, our own souls will be watered.

Remember, then, that as much as we need family and friends in our lives, they need us, as well. As much as they help us on our journeys toward destiny, they also need our help in fulfilling their own destinies. Never forget to treat others the way you yourself want to be treated as you head toward destiny.

Eleven

The Best-Kept Secret: Success

11
The Best-Kept Secret: Success

Then you will have good success.
—Joshua 1:8 (NKJV)

Have you ever heard of Wilma Rudolph, one of the greatest black track athletes of the twentieth century? Rudolph was born prematurely in 1940, the twentieth of twenty-two children. She faced a lot of obstacles from the time she took her first breath. Because she was born prematurely, Wilma was a frail little baby, and she soon suffered from sickness and disease. She spent most of her childhood in bed, plagued by mumps, measles, double pneumonia, scarlet fever, and chicken pox. The diseases left her feeble. Then, her parents noticed that her left leg was becoming deformed and losing its ability to function.

Wilma had polio. The doctor said she would never walk again. But Wilma's mother believed otherwise. She hauled Wilma back and forth to a hospital nearly fifty miles away twice a week for two years so that her little girl could get the treatment she needed. Finally, Wilma was able to limp around with the help of crutches and an iron brace on her bad leg. Wilma's parents and siblings then began to spend hours every day massaging her bad leg in hopes of stimulating healing in the weakened limb.

Wilma's family didn't stop at doing what they could for just her physical needs, either. They also continually encouraged her to believe in herself and her dreams. After many years of treatment and limping around with the iron brace, Wilma took off the brace and took her first steps without the aid of crutches. She began to run and play just like the other children her age. Soon, she was playing sports in school and, eventually, she began to excel in all that she did.

Wilma's desire to succeed carried her to college, where her track coach saw a gift in this young lady that was second to none. He trained her until she was one of the best runners in the United States and the world. Wilma competed in the Olympic Games in 1956 and 1960. In her second appearance at the Olympics, Wilma squared off against the greatest female runner of that time, a German named Yetta Mynie. Yetta had been unbeatable competition, but Wilma changed all that by beating her for the gold in the 100-meter and 200-meter races. Then, the two of them faced off in the 4x100-meter relay, where Wilma and Yetta served as anchors in the last leg of the race. When the batons were handed off to the anchors, Wilma dropped hers as Yetta sped off down the track. Wilma snatched up the baton and took off after Yetta. Yetta could only watch as Wilma passed her and captured the gold yet again. With the victory in the relay race, Wilma became the first American female to capture three gold medals at the Olympic Games. I have a lot of favorite success stories, but this one is most special to me because I wanted to be a track star at one point in my life.

I think any of us would consider Wilma Rudolph a success. The thing I admire most about Wilma is that she believed in herself and never gave up; her will to win pushed her to where she was the best at what she did. She also had a family who believed in her and supported her in the toughest of times, and she used that support to accomplish what no other woman had done at the Olympics up to that point. Now, few of us are probably going to go to the Olympics (but if that's a dream of yours, go for it!), but we all have the ability to be successful in this thing called life. Success, of course, can take many forms depending on whom you talk to. The most important question to answer for believers is, what does it mean to be a success in God's eyes?

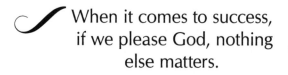

When it comes to success, if we please God, nothing else matters.

I believe being a success in God's eyes comes down to what Jesus called the two greatest commandments— loving God with all your heart, with all your soul, and with all your mind, and loving your neighbor as yourself (Matt. 22:37–39). If we are successful in fulfilling these two commandments, we can know without a doubt that we are accomplishing what God considers most important in the world. If we please God, nothing else matters when it comes to success.

Of course, if we are pleasing God, He will bless us in our lives here on earth. That might also mean being successful in the eyes of the world. It might mean having financial or material wealth. It might mean being in a position of power and authority. It might mean earning accolades and awards. But it also might not mean any of that. It might just mean that God blesses you by giving you the grace and wisdom to be a good husband or wife, mother or father. It might just mean that you are blessed with the ability to serve others in total obscurity, with no one ever noticing the job you do. Or it could mean you are blessed with the gift of intercession, and you labor in secret prayer for those around you.

The successes we can gain in life are obviously varied. However, the most important thing is that God wants us to be successful in our relationships with Him and others, as well as in the destiny He has planned for us. Of course, it's easy to *talk* about success. It's an entirely different thing to go out and *be* successful.

Get It

When it comes to "finding" success in life, we have to realize that we're not just going to trip over it some day as we go our merry way. No, we have to be tenacious in our attitudes toward success and destiny. Achieving our destinies demands that we be diligent, in the sight of God, in whatever we put our hands to. It means doing all the things we've talked about so far in this book.

I often think of my mom's philosophy of success. She used to say, "Nothing worth having in life is going to come looking for you. You must go look for it." How true that statement is. It reminds me of a passage in Scripture. In Matthew 11:12, Jesus said that *"the kingdom of heaven suffers violence, and the violent take it by force"* (NKJV). That's the kind of attitude I'm talking about when it comes to being successful in the kingdom of God on earth. We need to be forceful with all that we want to obtain in our spiritual walks, not surrendering to the world or sin or peer pressure or anything else that stands in the way of our relationships with God and our destinies. We need to stick with the plans God has for our lives, knowing that He has the perfect plans for us.

One way to view our paths to success is to remember that we are in a marathon, not a sprint. In a sprint, you get all pumped up, your adrenaline is rushing, and then you go out and do it. And it's over in a flash. Our lives with Christ and our paths to destiny are nothing like a sprint at all, even though some people act as though that's what they are. When such people are first saved, they are all pumped up, and they rush here and there doing all that they think God has called them to do. But eventually, the enthusiasm of being a new creature fades; it is at that point when they must realize that life in Christ and the path of destiny is a process. Eventually, the people who view destiny as a sprint and not a marathon will lose sight of God's plans for their lives and try to rely on their own strength to accomplish what they think will bring them success. That's not a good place to be in life because, just as in a sprint, when the race is over, the runners are gasping for breath and totally fatigued.

This is not how God wants us to look at our walks with Him as we move toward destiny. The way we can keep our enthusiasm for the race is by realizing that we are going to be in this thing for the long haul. This demands discipline and a determination to stick to God's plans for our lives, no matter what the cost. It means keeping our eyes on God through the most difficult of circumstances. It also means doing the things He calls us to do in the everyday drudgery of life. That's where we stumble the most, I think. We always want to do something great and extra just to keep up with everyone else. But God has called us to be faithful in doing what we are meant to do, even if those tings seem small and insignificant. Being faithful in a few things means that God will make you a ruler over many things on the path to destiny. (See Matthew 25:23.)

> Success in the eyes of the world is never certain, and failure in the eyes of God is never final.

Success is never easy to attain. But if we are doggedly determined to be successful in God's eyes, in our walk with Him, and in His destiny for our lives, then we will experience God's peace. God will be smiling down on us because we will be His true success stories.

Keep It

Now, once we've come to the place of success, we need to realize that no one can take it from us. Only we can destroy the success in our lives by neglecting the things that brought us success in the first place. The enemy can do all he wants to try to derail us, but it always comes down to our need to fight to stay successful in our paths to destiny. In addition, what looks like failure to us may not be. Let me explain what I mean by this. You may find yourself in a place where something you did comes crashing down around you. People in the world might shake their heads and think you're a failure. But success in the eyes of the world is never certain, and failure in the eyes of God is never final. Even when it appears as if you've failed in the natural, as long as you know you are in or have returned to God's will for your life, you can be sure that He is working all things together for your good and for your destiny.

So, make the determination that you will keep your success, no matter what happens in the natural. Declare that you will go on with God and your destiny despite what the world says about your "failure." I've heard it said that if you're going to fail, fail forward. In other words, if you stumble in life, stumble forward, regain your balance, and learn from your mistakes so that you can move on with your life.

Think about Moses. Again, here was a man who was a success in the eyes of the world. He was the adopted son of Pharaoh, and he lived the good life. But he became a fugitive wandering in the desert, then a shepherd. Now, in the eyes of the world, that would be quite a step down the ladder of success. But Moses was faithful where he was in life, and he found favor in God's eyes. God came to Moses and told him that he was going to be the deliverer of the Israelites. And that is exactly what Moses became. He went back to Egypt, and, with God's blessing and power, he helped liberate the entire Hebrew nation from enslavement to Pharaoh.

Even though it may have appeared that Moses' life had taken a turn for the worse, God was still in control. The key was that Moses remained faithful where he was in life. God blessed that faithfulness and moved Moses along to his ultimate destiny because of it. We need to do the same thing if we are to maintain success in God's eyes on our own path to destiny.

Of course, maintenance of our success takes a lot of work. It's similar to the regular maintenance of a house or car. There are little things we need to be continually doing to keep ourselves in line with the Word of God and His will for our lives. These are the basics of every-day Christianity that we discussed earlier. To maintain ourselves and our successes in our journeys to destiny, we need to be praying, reading and meditating on God's Word, practicing spiritual warfare, and fellowshipping with other believers. Doing these things helps maintain a strong spiritual foundation that we can build on for the rest of our lives. In this way, we can continue to achieve success in the pursuit of our destinies because the foundation has already been laid.

Fight for It

As I said before, the enemy will do all he can to bring apparent failure into your life so that he can detour you from destiny. He understands that as you become suc-cessful, you will further the kingdom of God. This idea obviously doesn't sit well with the devil, which is why he does so much to keep us from being successful in our relationship with God and successful on earth as we journey to our destinies.

I think that, too often, we take the reality of the devil too lightly. I'm not saying we should be looking for demons behind every bush. I'm also not saying that we should go blaming the devil for everything that seems to go wrong in our lives. What I am saying is that we need to understand we are spiritually at war. But our struggle is not against flesh and blood on this earth. It's against the rulers, principalities, powers, and spiritual wicked-ness in the heavenly realms. (See Ephesians 6:10–12.)

Destiny

The reality of our war against the kingdom of darkness is something we need to keep in mind as we move toward destiny. If we are to fight off the devil's attempts at stopping our success in life, we will have to do all we can to maintain our walks with God. We will need to die each day to self and crucify the flesh. We will need to daily declare Jesus as Lord of our lives. We will need to be ready to go where God leads us, even if it appears to be into failure. Remember, God has a plan for your life. He can and will work everything together for the successful achievement of your destiny here on earth. Keep trusting Him, and keep persevering in your success on the path of destiny in your life.

Twelve

Destiny Is Yours—Get Up and Go After It!

12

Destiny Is Yours—Get Up and Go After It!

Then Jesus said to him, "Get up!
Pick up your mat and walk."
—John 5:8 (NIV)

Many years ago, in Jerusalem, near the city entrance known as the Sheep Gate, there was a pool called Bethesda. There were large porches leading down into this pool. These porches were covered each day by the sick and disabled. Every so often, an angel would come down from heaven and stir the waters of the pool. Whoever made it into the rippling waters first would be healed of whatever disease he had.

A man who had been lame and bedridden for thirty-eight years was one of those who waited by the pool. Every time he saw the waters stirred, he laid there in his pain while someone else went to the water and received healing.

One day, the invalid was lying on his bed mat, waiting again for the waters to be stirred by an angel.

Suddenly, a man stood over him. He looked up as the man spoke to him.

"Do you want to get well?" the man asked him.

The invalid hung his head. "Sir, I have no one to help me into the pool when the water is stirred. While I am trying to get in, someone else goes down ahead of me."

The man looked at him and then exclaimed, "Get up! Pick up your mat and walk."

The invalid jumped up, amazed at the power he felt coursing through his once lifeless limbs. He grabbed his bed and looked for the man who had healed him, but he couldn't find him in the large crowd. Later, the man who had been healed was surprised to see his healer standing before him in the temple. After speaking with the healer, the man went his way, telling everyone who it was that had made him well. (See John 5:1–15.)

It was Jesus who had given the man new life!

And it's Jesus who will give us new life each day to walk the path of destiny for our lives.

Too often, we become like the invalid who was at the healing pool. We sit around in our self-pity, our weakness, our excuses, our pain, and we wonder why everyone else is getting blessed and we aren't. We think that, if our lives are ever going to move along, God will just have to do some miraculous thing to put our destinies in motion. But there is where our problem lies.

Destiny doesn't just show up on the doorstep one day and say, "Here I am! Now, you can get on with the wonderful life you've been waiting for!"

It's as if we expect God to hold our hands and pull us along to where He wants us to go. Don't get me wrong; He'll hold our hands every step of our lives. But once He points us in the direction we're meant to go, it's up to us to go out and take hold of our destiny. We have a large responsibility in whether or not we achieve all that God has planned for us. No one and nothing can stop our destinies if we are doing all we can to draw closer to God and to abide in His will and plan for us.

Consider again the invalid by the pool. Thirty-eight years of his life passed by while he remained in his "comfort zone" of pain and suffering. He had become used to it. It took an encounter with God to get the man moving. When he was finally put on the spot by Jesus, he rose up in faith and took hold of the life Christ offered him. Jesus asked him, "Do you *really* want a new life?" and he responded in faith. But he had to make the choice to believe in order for his life to change.

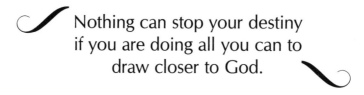

Nothing can stop your destiny
if you are doing all you can to
draw closer to God.

We have to make the same choice. Each day, we face the question from God, "Do you want to live today, or do you want to remain in the place of pain, in the place of self-pity, in the place of discouragement, where you are just a victim?" We must answer daily by faith, "I want to live!" It's our choice to make if we want to fulfill our destinies. Remember the old saying, "Destiny is not a matter of chance, it is a matter of choice; it is not a thing to be waited for, it is a thing to be achieved." Yes, there will be obstacles, and the enemy is going to do all he can to get you offtrack. But when you feel as if you just can't go on with your destiny anymore, or when you think all hope is lost because of some obstacle blocking your path, think about what we've talked about in this book.

Remember, whether or not you know your life's destiny, be faithful to God right now and believe in your destiny for today. Be sensitive to your talents, passions, and dreams, and wait patiently for God to reveal His plan for your life.

Also, never forget that change is inevitable in life. The people around you will change. The situations you are living in will change. If you are going to walk on your destined path, you will need to change along the way, too. But the pain of change can't be compared with becoming more Christlike and drawing closer to God and His will for your life; the pain is worth it.

Don't let your past decide your present or future. The past is the past. Learn from it, but don't let it hinder you on the way to your destiny. You have to live in the now, not getting stuck in what has been or dreaming too much about what will be. Serve God right now where you are with all you have, and seize the moment every chance you get. Always keep in mind that there is hope for the future as long as you abide in Christ and walk in His ways.

Remember also that everything that glitters in life is not gold. There will be those attractions in your life that will look like something good but, in the end, could prove to be fatal to your life's destiny if you yield to them. Be vigilant about who or what you allow into your life. Let the Lord lead you every step of the way, and He will keep you safe on the road to destiny.

If you face the bitter pill of betrayal in your life, remember that it can cripple your walk with God and your journey to destiny. Do not forget that God is with you, ready to help you walk in forgiveness and give you the grace to go on toward your destiny.

And always be watchful for what I consider to be the number one killer when it comes to destiny: fear. Fear can paralyze you, but remember that God did not give you a spirit of fear, but of power, love, and a sound mind (2 Tim. 1:7). You can overcome fear with faith. It's a battle, I know, but don't let fear stop you as you take hold of your destiny each day.

Remember, too, that your family and friends can be a vital support system to you. Learn to lean upon them when you need strength to go on. If you are not blessed with supportive family members or friends, keep praying to God to give you such people, and turn to your spiritual family in the body of Christ. Then, go on with your destiny, knowing that you can rely on God as your heavenly Father.

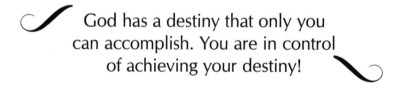

God has a destiny that only you can accomplish. You are in control of achieving your destiny!

As you continue along the path to destiny, be committed to your walk with God, and learn how to maintain success in every aspect of your life. Keep your destiny in your sights as you achieve every success, and let success carry you to fulfilling your destiny.

Dear brothers and sisters, don't wait any longer! God has a plan and purpose for your lives. He has a destiny that only you can accomplish. But He won't force it on you. Get up, and go after it! Remember that you have a large part in the fulfillment of you destiny. You are in control of achieving your destiny! Nothing can stand in the way of your destiny if you keep surrendering your life to God and abiding in Him.

If there's something holding you back from reaching your destiny, get over it, and then get on with it! Be like the invalid at the pool after he was healed. Jesus told him to take up his bed. That bed of sickness and pain was what held the man back for so long. So, take up the thing that is carrying you away from your destiny, and carry it with you as you move toward your destiny!

If Jesus was standing in front of you right now, He might very well say: "Get up! Get out of your comfort zone in life, and get moving! I'll be there to help you and to give you life. But take the first step in faith!"

It's your destiny.

Dream it.

Declare it.

Do it!

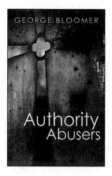

OTHER POWERFUL **B**OOKS
from Whitaker House

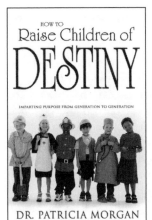

How to Raise Children of Destiny
Dr. Patricia Morgan

Dr. Patricia Morgan reveals the link between the rise of young prophets, priests, and kings in the body of Christ and the God-ordained heads of nations, spiritual leaders, and deliverers responsible for the salvation of a generation. Hear the call for godly parents to train their children to be the next generation of leaders and to teach them the strength and power that is found in the covenant promises of the God of their fathers!

ISBN: 0-88368-561-2 • Trade • 240 pages

The Battle for the Seed
Dr. Patricia Morgan

God has given one generation the ability to shape the next and thus shape the future, but He doesn't expect us to do it alone. Dr. Patricia Morgan shares what Scripture says about our children and how to raise a victorious generation. Discover how to parent with purpose, understanding the intent behind your child's design. We can't win the battle if we never confront the enemy. Join Dr. Morgan in *The Battle for the Seed!*

ISBN: 0-88368-560-4 • Trade • 128 pages

OTHER POWERFUL BOOKS
from Whitaker House

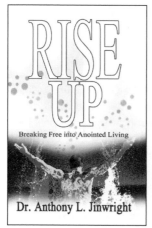

Rise Up: Breaking Free into Anointed Living
Dr. Anthony L. Jinwright

Your spiritual life seems more like a tedious chore than an energizing mission. You wonder how God's supernatural power can ever be yours. Can you ever live the God-directed, God-energized life? The answer is YES. Dr. Anthony L. Jinwright shares the secrets to living a vibrant, Spirit-empowered life. *Rise Up* and walk in the power of God!

ISBN: 0-88368-760-7 • Trade • 192 pages

Maximize Your Edge
Lance D. Watson

No roller coaster, race car, bungee cord, or game can give you the thrill that compares to the wild ups and downs of life. If your boat has been sunk a time or two, or if you've lost your passion for life, Lance Watson's practical, biblical strategies will help you navigate the complex game of life so that you'll not only survive, but you'll experience life like never before.

ISBN: 0-88368-714-3 • Trade • 240 pages

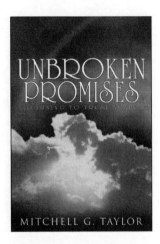

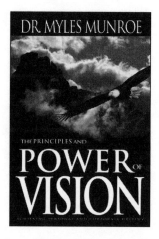